not on BOARD

JONAH'S PLUNGE INTO GOD'S PLAN

STEVE RICHARDSON

Not on Board: Jonah's Plunge Into God's Plan
by Steve Richardson

© 2024 Pioneers-USA
ISBN: 978-1-7352345-6-4

Edited by Maxine McDonald, Marti Wade, and Matt Green
Cover design: Karina Kolman
Author photo: Joseph Boyle

Contents

Praise for *Not on Board*

"What a delightful and potent shot of biblical truth so relevant for our time. Steve Richardson takes the rarely investigated Book of Jonah and digs up precious gems that perfectly fit our setting today. Let your mind and heart be stirred afresh by God's passion for the lost peoples of the world."

—Ivan Veldhuizen
Senior Vice President of Converge

"One of the gifts of *Not on Board* is the way that it awakens the reader to the sheer wonder of the God of Jonah and reminds us of how astounding His ways are and how astonishingly deep His compassion for the lost flows. The book subtly re-focuses our vision beyond the horizons of our all-too-familiar assumptions. Then it compels our hearts so that we too begin to catch sight of, and move towards, the boundless love and energy, the creativity and salvific purposes of our mighty Savior. There are some fine commentaries on Jonah, but, to my knowledge, none focus on the rich missiological subtext and even overt textual comment within the book. How can readers possibly not be enthused and energized about reaching the Ninevehs of our world?"

—Shelly J. Kearns
Pioneers Canada Board Chair

"After my 55 years of vocational missionary service, I have been (wrongly) tempted to conclude that I can 'ease up' on my involvement in the fulfillment of Christ's Great Commission. But not after reading this convicting (and encouraging) book! I hope you'll read it, too!"

—*Dr. George W. Murray, former President & Chancellor*
of Columbia International University

Dedication

To Ted Fletcher—father-in-law, mentor, and Pioneers founder—who, along with Peggy, traded in the American Dream for a heavenly calling. What a difference your obedience has made.

A Little Book of Big Ideas

In 1863, the most famous public speaker in America was a man named Edward Everett. During a much-anticipated keynote address, he delivered 13,000 words (about half the length of this book) in two hours without notes. Today, hardly anyone recognizes the name Edward Everett, let alone remembers what he said 150 years ago. But millions of Americans can quote from memory the opening line of the speech that followed immediately after Everett's: "Four score and seven years ago…"

Abraham Lincoln's 272-word Gettysburg Address conveyed more meaning and did it more memorably than Edward Everett's *tour de force*. Everett himself wrote to Lincoln the following day, "I wish that I could flatter myself that I had come as near to the central idea of the occasion in two hours as you did in two minutes."[1]

The Bible is a long book, but it is crafted with intense linguistic economy. Every word matters. Take the account of Creation, for example, or the Ten Commandments, the Beatitudes, or the Golden Rule. They convey so much about God and life in relatively little space. Even the more detailed and seemingly repetitive biblical narratives are still deliberate, without verbal excess, considering the diversity of intended audiences that span geography, culture, circumstance, and time. Imagine writing a book for an audience of "everyone." The Bible is as relevant to an Ethiopian eunuch in the first-century government of Queen Candace as it is to an Amazonian tribesman or a Wall Street executive 2,000 years later. As we read Scripture, we often wish to know more. Yet, God's Word is as intentional in what it *doesn't* say as in what it *does* say. God knows how much information we can responsibly manage. That's part of the miracle of His remarkable book.

Placed strategically near the end of the Old Testament is the account of a man named Jonah. His story summarizes what has happened up to that point in redemptive history and foreshadows what is yet to come. The Book of Jonah is an example of literary density. It is so short that you might miss it if you're not careful. In just 48 verses and 980 words of ancient Hebrew text, Jonah weaves threads of human fallibility into a spectacular tapestry of divine intentionality and grace.

I will admit to taking this episode in Israel's history for granted in the past or viewing it as just a well-used Sunday School text. Over time, however, I noticed that Jonah's story wasn't being taught as often as I had assumed. And when it was taught, the book's global message was often underappreciated. The deeper I mined in the text, the more I noticed veins of gold as relevant today as they were 2,750 years ago. Jonah is now one of my favorite books of the Bible (if favorites are allowed).

For one thing, the Jonah text is a work of literary

genius. Its two halves echo each other. Each half of the story involves a word from God (Jonah 1:1-2 and 3:1-2), an encounter with pagans (1:3-16 and 3:3-10), and a "crucial conversation" between Jonah and God (1:17-2:10 and 4:1-11). The book's central event is the recommissioning of God's messenger in Jonah 3:1-2.[2]

If this were not remarkable enough, we also find that each half of the book is chiastic in structure. The sequence of concepts in chapters 1 and 3 are repeated in reverse order in chapters 2 and 4, respectively, with the main ideas highlighted as the "hinges" in the middle. The central point of the first two chapters of Jonah is the sailors fearing the Lord. The hinge of the second half is the Ninevite king fearing the Lord. These layers of mirrored sequences, each with a central thought, blend together to emphasize the central command of the book: "Go to the great city of Nineveh and proclaim to it the message I give you" (Jonah 3:2).

More fundamentally, though, this two-page masterpiece invites us into the undomesticated heart of God. Its themes reverberate through the rest of Scripture: God is supremely (even shockingly) sovereign, just, and loving. Salvation comes from Him. He calls His people to align their hearts with His and to join His mission in the compassionate pursuit of a world hurtling toward oblivion.

Some take the story as an allegory. I read it as a factual account of historical events, as Jesus did (Matthew 12:39-41). The Book of Jonah summarizes, in testimonial form, a millennium of redemptive history, the challenge of staying "mission true," and the essence of the gospel in the suffering and triumph of the Messiah.

Not on Board

My intention here is not to provide a detailed exegetical study of Jonah. Others are more qualified for that, and many resources are available. Instead, my goal is to highlight the big-picture themes that I hope will illuminate and energize our shared pursuit of God's glory on the global stage. Join me on the adventure Jonah did his best to avoid and discover the power and mercy of the God of Surprises.

CHAPTER 1

A Surprising God

"For my thoughts are not your thoughts,
neither are your ways my ways," declares the LORD.
"As the heavens are higher than the earth,
so are my ways higher than your ways
and my thoughts than your thoughts."
—Isaiah 55:8-9

Do you like surprises? My instinctive response is always yes. But then I wonder, *Wait a minute, what kind of surprise are we talking about?*

When I was 18 months old, my family's motorized canoe capsized in a tea-colored New Guinea river full of crocodiles. We were fortunate to all survive.[3] My brother heard a rustling sound in his bedroom one night in that same jungle. Searching the small room with his flashlight, he found an eight-foot python about to make a meal of our newborn kittens. The snake had carried them down the hall from the pantry one by one and was covering them with saliva in preparation for a feast. Those aren't the sort of surprises we welcome! On the other hand, most of us appreciate an impromptu birthday party, word of a new grandchild on the way, or news that someone has unexpectedly included us in their will.

The Pull of Predictability

While we may occasionally enjoy a good surprise, a key feature of human nature is the powerful drive to predict and control outcomes: our environment, health, schedule, finances, food (*That's not medium rare!*), and even the weather (*Will it rain this afternoon? How long and how hard?*). Our whole worldview is wrapped around the notion of anticipating and manipulating our circumstances. To a point, this is a natural, God-given capacity and responsibility to "fill the earth and subdue it. Rule over the fish in the sea and the birds in the sky and over every living creature that moves on the ground" (Genesis 1:28). But, as we see in Eden, we are always in danger of trying to usurp God's role by taking control over things that are rightfully His alone.

In reality, it's almost always in unexpected situations that we learn the most about God and ourselves. When life follows my plans and meets my expectations, I may enjoy feeling secure and relaxed, but I'm probably not growing. Perhaps that's one reason why God has a beautiful, unnerving, exhilarating, and sometimes frustrating way of surprising us, again and again, with His superior (but not necessarily comfortable) plan. While God is consistent in His character, from a human standpoint, He often strikes us as unpredictable in His methods. Words often attributed to Charles West sum it up well: "We turn to God for help when our foundations are shaking, only to learn that it is God who is shaking them."

All of us can point to game-changing events and conversations that have shaped our lives. As a missionary kid, I contracted a bad case of hepatitis in seventh grade and missed the whole school year. While difficult and not what I would have chosen, that year turned out to be spiritually formative for me. Then, after tenth grade, our family moved from Canada to California. The transition affected the entire course of my life. A couple of years later, when I was a senior in a Pasadena high school, my father returned home from a ministry trip and announced out of the blue, "Steve, I met a young lady that I think would be perfect for you." And sure enough, I married that young lady four years later! God has almost certainly introduced unexpected inflection points in your journey as well. He is, after all, the master of surprise.

A Book of Surprises

God is the most creative Person in the universe, so it makes sense that He has packed the Bible full of surprises. It's an astonishing book from cover to cover. Nearly every page would shock us if it weren't so familiar. Scripture contains so many unexpected events and ideas that some readers relegate it to the genre of myth and fable. A global deluge decimates the earth, except for one man and his family. Fortunately, they just spent 50 years building a big boat to save themselves and the planet's animal life. Hundreds of thousands of slaves escape on a 40-year journey through the desert, plundering their oppressors on their way out of town after a series of nation-crippling plagues. A shepherd poet kills a giant with a slingshot and becomes king. Daniel gets a decent night's sleep in a pit full of hungry lions. A peasant girl named Esther becomes queen of Persia while the prime minister is hung on the gallows he prepared for her cousin.

Jesus' birth is a huge surprise to almost everyone, including His own mother. Virtually everything He says surprises His listeners. So does His death, even though He repeatedly predicted it. Then Jesus shocks His followers (as well as the guards and religious authorities) by rising from the dead. I expect His Second Coming to also be a big surprise, even for those of us anticipating it. And these are just a few examples among hundreds.

Considering the Bible's countless surprises, I propose a new field of study—"surprisology." And, while we're at it, let's add a new name for God to our lexicon: "God the Surpriser." As we study His Word, let's ask the key question, "What things surprise me, or *should* surprise me, in this text?" Our wonder or dismay at God's actions and self-revelation in Scripture can help us identify gaps in our understanding of His nature and purposes.

When I was a child, my family had a tradition of opening one present on Christmas Eve. We had to wait until morning for the rest. My brothers would instinctively go for the larger gifts, but I soon learned to take my chances on the smaller packages. They often contained the best presents. One year, I opened a pocket-sized gift to find a solar-powered calculator. Its few basic functions were advanced technology at the time. I was amazed at all the technological wizardry lying in the palm of my hand. The Book of Jonah is just like that. In a Bible full of thousands of surprises, Jonah stands out as a small package with some especially consequential insights for God's people:

Life for Jonah [is] a series of disconcerting surprises and frustrations. He tries to escape from God and is trapped. He then gives up, accepts the inevitability of perishing, and is saved. He obeys when given a second chance, and is frustratingly, embarrassingly successful.[4]

I want to explore four key surprises Jonah encountered as he ventured reluctantly into the heart of God. I think of these as four lessons God used to draw Jonah into a deeper awareness of His purposes and a greater participation in His mission. Before plunging into the drama, let's set the stage.

Jonah Before the Whale

If you aren't familiar with the story of "Jonah and the whale," it only takes about ten minutes to read. The book begins in Israel during a time of prosperity[5] and apostasy, which frequently go together. Seasons of prosperity often represent a greater threat to our spiritual vitality than seasons of hardship. Jonah's adventures take place long after the division of the nation of Israel into two kingdoms, most likely during the reign of Jeroboam II (782-753 B.C.).[6] Decades later, the Assyrian army will take the northern kingdom into captivity. Jonah is from Gath Hepher (2 Kings 14:25), just north of Nazareth, Jesus' hometown. The Pharisees must have forgotten about him when they claimed no prophet had come from Galilee (John 7:52).[7]

Jonah is first mentioned in 2 Kings 14:25, where he prophesies that God will graciously restore the land to Israel, even though Jeroboam II has acted wickedly. Perhaps that incident is an example to Jonah of God's graciousness to people who don't deserve it.[8] Either way, Jonah experiences the best of prophethood: God gives him a positive message for Israel and fulfills it dramatically in short order. It's possible Jonah became a folk hero as a result. After all, who doesn't like a prophet who predicts good fortune?

But then, suddenly, Jonah's life takes an unexpected turn. Other prophets have delivered oracles against foreign nations and spent time outside their homelands. But Jonah has the unwelcome distinction of being the first—and only—prophet of Israel specifically sent abroad to preach directly to a distant country.[9] And not just any country. To Assyria. Israel's archenemy.

The immorality and violence of the Assyrian empire has reached a red-alert level, and God is sending Jonah to one of their leading cities, Nineveh, to deliver an ultimatum. No more happy, comforting messages of victory for the home team. From a human point of view, the Ninevites will most likely reject Jonah's message and kill the messenger. After all, the story is set in an era when human rights are not prioritized. Life is cheap, and "free speech" isn't so free, especially on enemy territory. Alternatively, Nineveh could accept the message and be spared from destruction. Neither option is attractive to Jonah.

A Promise of Astounding Proportions

To appreciate God's message to the Ninevites and Jonah's reaction to it, we need to understand God's long-term plan and His intended role for Israel in its interactions with neighboring cultures. We find the key right where we would expect it, back in the "beginning." Genesis chapters

1-11 function as a vital introduction to the Bible. They deal with the world as a whole—from its Creation and Fall, the growth of the population and of evil, and God's judgment in the Flood. Then, a similar cycle starts with Noah's descendants. "The earth" is a frequent refrain in these opening chapters. Genesis 10 records a list of 70 nations, symbolizing totality or completeness, descending from Noah's three sons and migrating to Africa, Europe, and Asia. Genesis 11 further describes the proliferation of peoples and languages following the construction of Babel.

The stage is set. The dilemma is clear. The main storyline of the Bible (God's solution for the intractable problem of sin and mankind's lostness) gets underway in chapter 12. Abram is, presumably, minding his own business as a middle-class suburbanite living in the Mesopotamian metropolis of Ur. Suddenly, God interrupts his routine with a radical call and a promise. We refer to this promise as the Abrahamic Covenant.

God's recorded conversation with Abram is short, just three verses long. And it is one way, with God speaking to Abram. Yet this brief declaration stands among the most important surprises of all time. It is arguably the key to understanding all subsequent redemptive history. God launches Abram away from his home into life as a nomad in search of a homeland, declaring in Genesis 12:2-3,

> I will make you into a great nation,
>   and I will bless you;
> I will make your name great,
>   and you will be a blessing.
> I will bless those who bless you,

> and whoever curses you I will curse;
>   and all peoples on earth
>   will be blessed through you.

With this promise, God has bound Himself to a course of action that, over time, will have a world-changing impact. He even changes Abram's name to Abraham to reflect the magnitude of the promise. "Abram" means exalted father. "Abraham" means father of a *multitude*. Later, God says this multitude will be as uncountable as the stars, the sand, and the dust (Genesis 13:16, 22:17).

The idea that God would present Himself as a source of blessing to Abraham isn't particularly surprising at first glance. Even in Abraham's day, everyone curried the favor of his or her god, usually through sacrifices. People didn't think about having a personal relationship with a deity in any wholesome sense. The gods were capricious and didn't care about people as individuals. To the extent that they did, it was a cause for concern, not comfort. But here, God is not talking exclusively about ordinary blessings like rain, health, and safety. As we learn later in passages like Galatians 3:8, God is announcing, in advance, a vast array of benefits associated with the gospel of Jesus Christ and citizenship in His kingdom. Time will reveal a lot more about these words than Abraham could have imagined at the time.

Consider some of the other surprises embedded in this three-verse conversation:

- God takes the initiative, not Abraham. God is not responding to sacrifices or some kind of human request. He invades Abraham's world uninvited.

- God's promises are explicit, detailed, and concrete. God promises Abraham genetic descendants, a nation, a homeland, and a purpose outside himself.
- God is calling Abraham out of an idolatrous family and culture into a radical monotheism (see Joshua 24:2 and Genesis 31:19).
- God is initiating a covenant relationship, not just a command, idea, or aspiration. The Creator voluntarily binds Himself with an unbreakable oath. The solemnity of this oath is reinforced later in Scripture (Hebrews 6:13-20).

God has the whole world in mind when making His covenant with Abraham. No other god ever initiated a plan encompassing the entire planet. Gods were territorial. People negotiated personal and regional arrangements with them, not visions of global proportions.

The scope of the promise is breathtaking—way beyond just a good harvest or a healthy baby. It extends to the ends of the earth, and its fulfillment will span millennia, setting the stage for eternity. This plan involves thousands of years and billions of people (Isaiah 11:9-10).

The promise requires a faith response in practical terms. Abraham has to get up, collect his wife and a few relatives, and start a journey.

Essentially, God tells Abraham, "I want to bless you beyond your wildest dreams." But He doesn't stop there. At best, any other god would say, "I will bless you and curse your enemies," and there's certainly an element of that. Those who curse Abraham will find that their curses boomerang back on themselves. But God adds a breathtaking assertion, "All the nations on earth will be blessed through you." Abraham and his descendants are being called for a very special purpose. They are to be a conduit of God's saving power for the world. God has not forgotten "the earth" of the prior 11 chapters of Genesis. On the contrary, He is launching a long-term, costly initiative to save the world. Abraham's descendants, the nation of Israel, will inherit a multi-layered blessing and responsibility, including descendants, a homeland, a reputation, custodianship of God's self-revelation, and an identity as God's holy people. The purpose of all this is to display to the nations God's glory, power, and saving grace (Exodus 19:5-6). Israel is to be a "kingdom of priests" through whom the world's Messiah will someday come. It is to stand in the gap on behalf of all the nations. In Jonah's day, more than a thousand years after the Abrahamic Covenant, those nations include Assyria.

A Nation of Recalcitrant Priests

At times throughout its history, Israel fulfilled its role as a channel of blessing to the nations. The effect was astounding. Think of the Psalms, sung first by Israel and now used in worship by hundreds of millions of people worldwide. Israel's Exodus, the conquest of Canaan, and its "golden age" during the reigns of King David and King Solomon were a testimony to surrounding nations. Solomon's prayer during the dedication of the temple (1 Kings 8:41-43) is a classic example:

> As for the foreigner who does not belong to your people Israel but has come from a distant land because of your name—for they will hear of your great name and your mighty hand and your

outstretched arm—when they come and pray toward this temple, then hear from heaven, your dwelling place. Do whatever the foreigner asks of you, so that all the peoples of the earth may know your name and fear you, as do your own people Israel, and may know that this house I have built bears your Name.

Or consider the queen of Sheba witnessing Solomon's majesty and recognizing the Lord as the source of his wealth and wisdom (1 Kings 10:6-9). These and other bright spots are highlighted in the pages of Scripture, but they are relatively rare over the long span of Israel's history.

The Jewish people were generally much more interested in the "top line" of the Abrahamic Covenant ("I will bless you") than they were in the "bottom line" ("All peoples on earth will be blessed through you"). For generations, they failed to honor the Lord, to keep the Sabbath, and to live righteously as a testimony to the nations around them. God's patience eventually ran out, and both Israel and Judah were brutally conquered and carried away into exile. God described His anger and heartbreak through the prophet Ezekiel (Ezekiel 36:17-21):

"[W]hen the people of Israel were living in their own land, they defiled it by their conduct and their actions. ... So I poured out my wrath on them because they had shed blood in the land and because they had defiled it with their idols. I dispersed them among the nations, and they were scattered through the countries. ... And wherever they went among the nations they profaned my holy name, for it was said of them, 'These are the

LORD's people, and yet they had to leave his land.'
I had concern for my holy name, which the people
of Israel profaned among the nations where they
had gone."

The story of Jonah is a microcosm of Israel's reluc-
tance to embrace its priestly, intercessory role. Instead of
being an example of righteousness, it had to be disciplined
by the nations it was intended to bless. One Bible scholar
explains the relationship between Jonah and the Abrahamic Covenant this way:

> The Lord's love for the souls of all people was
> supposed to be mediated through Israel, God's
> elect and covenant nation. Through Israel the
> blessing of His compassion was to be preached to
> the nations (Isaiah 49:3). The Book of Jonah was
> a reminder to Israel of her missionary purpose.
> ... Though Israel was unfaithful in its missionary
> task, God was faithful in causing His love to be
> proclaimed. ... Jonah's spiritual hardness illus-
> trated and rebuked Israel's callousness.[10]

Israel had become a spiritually stagnant pond rather
than a life-giving river. In failing to bless others, it forfeited
much of its own blessing. It's a principle of God's kingdom.
Those who refuse to share what they've received end up
losing what they have.

Embracing the God of Surprises

Have you thought much about the fact that God's promise
to Abraham is still in process, and your life is a part of its
fulfillment? Many individuals and communities today have

yet to hear about the blessing of God's provision for their sins through Jesus. More than 40 percent of the world's population doesn't know that a descendant of Abraham made a way for them to be reconciled to their Creator.[11]

Jonah isn't a story about a big fish. It can't be. The fish is only mentioned in three verses. I don't think it's fundamentally even a story about Jonah. This book is a message about God and His heart, which contrasts with the lives and attitudes of His people. Through Jonah's story, God reveals what He thinks about people who don't know Him, who He might use to change that, the response of the world to God's message of mercy, and the impact it can have on the messenger.

It's an important message not just for Jonah's contemporaries in Israel but also for us today. We may consider ourselves quite different from Jonah and more sophisticated than the people to whom the story was initially directed. But are we really that different? We, too, may be out of alignment in our values and priorities. In a sense, Jonah's experience is more for our benefit than for his. Through his recorded story, millions of people across the ages have had an opportunity to wrestle with uncomfortable truths regarding God's character. They have been faced with difficult choices on how to respond. Let's listen to Jonah's testimony with humility.

Not everyone wants to be surprised, even by God. Many of us are quite content to live within the confines of what we know and think we can control. But if the Holy Spirit is drawing you toward the mysterious plan that He is carefully unfolding, then this little book is for you. Join me in praying with child-like faith and maybe a healthy dose of trepidation, "Lord, surprise me today with Your superior plan."

Discussion Questions

1. Do you like surprises?
2. How has God surprised you, either recently or in your past?
3. What do you find most surprising about the way God acts and describes Himself in the Bible?
4. How has God fulfilled the "top line" of the Abrahamic Covenant ("I will bless you")? What about the "bottom line" ("All peoples on earth will be blessed through you")?
5. How content are you with your current involvement in God's global mission? Are you hesitant, willing, or eager to be surprised by how God may want to use you?

CHAPTER 2

An Unthinkable Mission

*The word of the LORD came to Jonah son of
Amittai: "Go to the great city of Nineveh and
preach against it, because its wickedness has come
up before me." —Jonah 1:1-2*

J onah's adventure begins with an explosive command: "Get
up, go to Nineveh, and preach a message of judgment."
Can you feel Jonah's shock? Can you imagine God personally commanding you to preach in the streets of Baghdad,
Beijing, or Barcelona? There is no "should you choose to
accept it" clause attached to this impossible mission.

At first glance, it appears that Jonah is being sent with
a message of condemnation. God gives him a seemingly
straightforward assignment related to Nineveh: "Preach
against it" (Jonah 1:2). Exposing sin was a core aspect of a
prophet's calling, and the biblical writer makes no mention
here of a second chance for Nineveh. And so, we may be
surprised to discover at the end of the book that God spares
the city and its inhabitants.

Our reluctant prophet, however, knows better. He is not
surprised by God's mercy. He anticipates it, and he doesn't
like it. Later, Jonah explains his reason for disobeying God

Not on Board

in his own words: "I knew that you are a gracious and compassionate God, slow to anger and abounding in love, a God who relents from sending calamity" (Jonah 4:2). He is quoting Exodus 34:6 (and similar passages), where God describes Himself to Moses. Among God's primary attributes are His love and compassion. Why would God bother to warn a city of coming judgment unless there remained a possibility that He would relent?

As a missionary kid who attended boarding school, I've always taken comfort in the compassion of God. I knew He would be with me through the months of separation from my parents. Still today, I frequently remind myself that I serve a loving God. It's a core part of the gospel. Somehow, Jonah doesn't seem to find God's compassion very comforting, at least not when it is directed toward Nineveh. The scale and the scope of God's mercy greatly unnerves him.

When Jonah runs away, it isn't to spare Nineveh from doom. More likely, he intends to ensure that their doom is sealed. Judging by his explanation at the end of the book, Jonah would have been willing (perhaps even eager) to relay a message of condemnation to Nineveh if there had been no possibility of mercy. Jonah is surprised—and indignant—that God cares about a nation he fears and despises. Isn't Exodus 34:6 followed by another equally important aspect of God's character: "He does not leave the guilty unpunished"? As we will see in a moment, the Ninevites certainly qualified as guilty. Shouldn't mercy have reasonable limits?

Why Jonah Ran

Jonah had some obvious reasons for not being excited to preach in Nineveh. As previously noted, he may have been a hero in Israel during a time of relative prosperity. Maybe he had a pretty good life and ministry as it was. He wasn't looking for a new assignment. Perhaps he had a wife and kids to consider, fields to cultivate, or a business to run. And getting to Nineveh wouldn't be an easy journey. It would take Jonah longer to get to Nineveh, with far more risks, than it would take you or me to get almost anywhere in the world today. And how would he frame his message? What if the Ninevites didn't understand his Aramaic accent? Practical and logistical concerns like these might dominate our thinking if we were in a similar situation. But there's more.

Nineveh was among the world's largest and most intimidating cities during Jonah's lifetime. God Himself called it a "great city" (Jonah 4:11). Nineveh was founded by Nimrod and is symbolic of the world system in opposition to God (Genesis 10:8-12).[12] It was located near present-day Mosul, Iraq.[13] In places, Nineveh's walls may have been 100 feet high and wide enough to race three chariots side-by-side. They may have stretched as much as 60 miles around the city.[14] Nineveh housed somewhere between 120,000 and 600,000 people, depending on how Jonah 4:11 is interpreted (maybe as large as present-day Baltimore).[15]

The Assyrians also had a fearsome reputation for brutality and torture. One historian describes them this way:

> The Assyrian kings literally tormented the world.
> … they made pyramids of human heads; they

sacrificed holocausts of the sons and daugh-
ters of their enemies; ... they impaled "heaps of
men" on stakes, and strewed the mountains and
choked the rivers with dead bones; they cut off the
hands of kings, and nailed them on the walls, ...
and covered pillars with the flayed skins of rival
monarchs.[16]

Nineveh's kings even boasted about their cruelty in
monuments commemorating their victories in battle. Some
of those carvings depict acts of torture, including skinning
people alive, and are on display at the British Museum.[17]
And the Assyrians were idolaters. The prophet Nahum
would later describe their wickedness and call them "vile"
(Nahum 1:14, 3:1-4).

Prophesying destruction to a pagan emperor known for
torturing his enemies is no small matter. Few of us have
embraced a ministry role that came with a decent chance
of being skinned alive and turned into wallpaper. Jonah
had good reason to be afraid to go to Nineveh, much less
to preach there. But Jonah didn't say he ran because he
was afraid of the Assyrians. He ran away "lest the compassion of God should spare the sinful city in the event
of its repenting."[18]

Assyria's wickedness and cruelty and the threat it posed
to Israel must have made Nineveh seem to Jonah to be an
especially unworthy recipient of God's compassion. About
30 years after the reign of Jeroboam II ended, in 722 B.C.,
Assyria turned its wrath on Jonah's homeland. They invaded
the northern kingdom of Israel as God's instrument of judgment. We cannot be certain if Jonah knew about Assyria's

impending role in Israel's demise at the time of his call to Nineveh, but he likely had a good idea of what lay ahead. Assyria had already threatened to conquer Israel at least once.[19] The prophet Hosea, whose ministry overlapped with Jonah's, named Assyria as the instrument of Israel's judgment (Hosea 9:3). At the very least, Jonah knew God would use Israel's enemies to discipline the nation for its ongoing unfaithfulness.[20]

Jonah may have thought, *If Assyria's wickedness has reached a crucial threshold and they're going to come under judgment, can we not just get on with it? If I warn them and they repent, it will just give them more time to become a sharper knife.* From Jonah's perspective, the situation was horribly unjust. Here he was, a prophet of Israel, being told to give a cruel, foreign nation an opportunity to extend its lifespan. It would be like giving a violent criminal a "get out of jail free card." It felt wrong, and Jonah wanted no part of it.

In Defense of Jonah

I think we sometimes give Jonah short shrift. It is possible he was more advanced in his understanding of God's heart than many of us. How deeply do we wrestle with the tension between God's mercy and His justice? What about the destiny of entire peoples and nations? Or issues of societal decay and judgment and our responsibility in that mix? Our God systematically makes people deeply uncomfortable as they get to know Him better. When was the last time your awareness of God's sovereignty, His plan, and His intentions for each of us made you nervous? Jonah didn't have the benefit of understanding God's redemptive vision in nearly as much detail as we do today. And yet, he understood something important about God's compassion.

We find powerful linguistic symbolism in Jonah's story. His name means "dove." His father is called Amittai, which means "truth" or "faithfulness." Joppa means "beautiful" in Hebrew. Nineveh signified chaos, rebellion, and idolatry in the Jewish mind. Tarshish, on the other hand, was a sort of Garden of Eden associated with gold, silver, ivory, apes, and baboons (1 Kings 10:22-25). Jonah, a man of peace entrusted with a heritage of truth, doesn't accept God's mission to a chaotic world. Instead, he heads toward a beautiful place where he can enjoy peace and prosperity. It's a picture not only of Israel but of how many Christians live today. We also want to avoid the chaos associated with God's mission to a rebellious world.

Jonah didn't just ignore God and stay home. He expressed his disagreement candidly by packing his bag and going down to Joppa. Then he left for Tarshish, which was no easy undertaking. While Nineveh was located about 600 miles northeast of Israel, most scholars agree that Tarshish sat about 2,500 miles to the west, on the southern coast of Spain.[21] The voyage would have been long, dangerous, and expensive. King Solomon's navy required three years to make a similar round trip (1 Kings 10:22).

Jonah's flight wasn't a rash act or a prophetic temper tantrum. He must have thought long and hard before he uprooted his entire life, both physically and spiritually, to avoid delivering God's message to Nineveh. I imagine he had to sell land to pay for the fare. He had to explain why he was leaving to his friends and family (and possibly even the king of Israel). And Jonah likely didn't intend to return. His disagreement with God was so strong that he was willing to abandon his calling as a prophet and go into self-imposed exile on the perimeter of the known world. Now, that is true conviction!

Jonah may have inferred that because God intended to offer mercy to Nineveh, He would be less merciful to Israel, as if God's compassion came in limited supply. He was also aware that Israel itself had received warnings from his fellow prophets. Wasn't Assyria far worse? Jonah wanted God to judge Assyria and bless Israel. God offered mercy to both nations. He had sent prophet after prophet to warn His chosen people that their unfaithfulness was leading them toward destruction. Now, he was sending just one prophet to Nineveh with the same message, and even that seemed too much to Jonah.

Perhaps it's hard for us to relate to Jonah's resentment of the Assyrians because, in the West, most of us don't live with the same fear of enemy invasion. Oceans separate us from most of the rest of the world, and we don't perceive ourselves as having enemies in the same sense that Israel did. We may have concerns about terrorists or intercontinental ballistic missiles, but I don't think many of us feel like we're on the verge of being invaded by a foreign ruler who will burn our cities, put hooks in our noses, and drag any survivors into slavery. To most of us, wars are things that happen in distant places. Modern economic and even geopolitical threats don't have quite the same psychological impact as pyramids of severed heads.

But in Jonah's day, Israel was a small nation surrounded

by violent superpowers. And from one perspective, Jonah was right about the danger of sparing Nineveh. The spiritual turning died out within 50 years. Jonah might have lived to see Assyria take the northern kingdom into exile, although he would have been an old man then. The northern kingdom was never re-established. It was game over.

Let's have some sympathy for Jonah because his fears were real, and he acted on his convictions. And yet, he missed the point. God loved Assyria. In His mercy, He extends compassion even to the undeserving. He makes the sun shine on everyone, believer and unbeliever alike, and He offers salvation to everyone.

What About Us?

I'm comforted that sharing our spiritual blessings with the rest of the world is God's idea. It doesn't come naturally to us humans. God is carrying out His Abrahamic promise as part of a master strategy. The challenge is, like Jonah, we have ideas that often conflict with God's. We want Him to fall into line with our plan. Or we try to run away and leave God—and His instructions—behind us. Without an appreciation for the big-picture context of what God is doing in the world, we will be perpetually frustrated. His actions (and inactions) don't make sense unless we accept them in faith as part of a global, eternal plan.

Jonah and most of the Israelites were self-absorbed. God intended them to be whole-hearted worshippers and conduits of His blessing to surrounding people groups. And he intends that for us today—arguably even more so, given the increased breadth and depth of our understanding of His redemptive plan.

Let's be honest. How do we score on God's scale of compassion? Are there people we deem, consciously or not, to be unworthy of the same level of grace that we have received? Do we viscerally feel that God loves both our neighbors down the street and the Bedouin nomad in the Sahara Desert as much as He loves us? And how much do we value God's grace toward us if we consider others less worthy to share in it, or ourselves not obligated to convey it? We probably never actually think, *This person should not receive God's mercy.* We probably agree, cognitively, that everyone should hear the gospel message and have an opportunity to repent and find new life in Christ. That's commendable as a starting point, but I don't think it's where God wants to leave us.

A mark of our authenticity as followers of Jesus is our concern for the "lost sheep"—people separated from God. Jonah had 600 miles to traverse to warn Nineveh, but people can be far from the gospel in many ways besides geography. Social constraints, caste systems, economic disparity, historical resentments and injustices, political distinctions, linguistic chasms, and differences in worldview all make it difficult for people to learn of God's justice and compassion and respond with repentance. Gospel emissaries today attempt to cross vast spiritual distances to reach people all over the world who have no idea what they're talking about when they try to explain that Jesus died on the Cross to save them. As one of my mentors used to say, "This is the hardest work in the world." It's also incredibly fulfilling and God-glorifying work!

A Call to Headhunters

My own family's story is a more recent example of the Nineveh mandate at work. In 1962, when I was six months old, my parents and I left Vancouver, Canada, on a ship called the Oriana. We traveled to what was then Netherlands New Guinea, the western half of the world's second-largest island. New Guinea looks like a Tyrannosaurus rex basking on the equator just north of Australia, with a mountainous spine stretching from head to tail. When we arrived, the established missionaries told my parents, "We've just heard about a tribe down in the malaria-infested southern swamps. They're called the Sawi. We don't know much about them except that they live in treehouses and are probably head-hunters. Are you willing to take the gospel to them?"

I like to think that my parents considered my interests at least briefly before they responded, "We'd love to." We settled into a little thatch-roofed house in the Sawi jungle. As my parents began learning the language, they were shocked to find that the Sawi were not only cannibals but also ideal-ized treachery. When my father eventually told the story of Jesus, including how He was betrayed to death by His friend Judas, one of the men chuckled. "Tell us more about Judas," he said. "He sounds like one of us! I would love to give my daughter in marriage to a man like Judas."

My father's heart sank as he realized he had a major cross-cultural communication challenge on his hands. How could the Sawi ever understand the gospel message if they considered Judas the hero?

The answer came a few months later in the form of

another surprising cultural concept, the securing of peace between warring Sawi villages through the giving of a *tarop tim*, or "peace child." This event's subsequent drama and impact are vividly documented in my father's missionary classic *Peace Child*.[22] In time, a significant percentage of the Sawi people came to saving faith in Jesus. They formed an alliance with their former enemies to share the gospel with other language groups in the jungle and now worship together in vibrant churches.

My parents, like many missionaries throughout history, stepped out in obedience at significant risk to themselves to warn a godless society of divine judgment and God's offer of salvation through His own Peace Child. Growing up with a front-row seat, I witnessed the truth of Romans 1:16, "The gospel ... is the power of God that brings salvation to everyone who believes: first to the Jew, then to the Gentile," and even to isolated cannibal tribes like the Sawi!

Modern-Day Ninevehs

While we may readily imagine God's call to a cannibalistic jungle tribe as being a kind of "Nineveh experience," many other barriers can separate whole communities and societies from the blessings of the gospel. Think of the 7,000-plus languages spoken worldwide (not to mention thousands of dialects). Many of them still need Bible translations so that people can understand God's Word. Or think of the geographic and cultural obstacles encountered in places like Tibet and Yemen. I have friends who ride camels from oasis to oasis with nomadic tribes in the Chadian Sahel. Others serve among committed atheists in Europe or immigrant communities like the Uyghurs in American cities.

Many of today's gospel ambassadors don't live in remote rural areas but rather in the "great cities" of the world. God has a particular concern and place in His heart for these massive concentrations of humanity. Whereas less than 10 percent of the world's population lived in cities throughout most of history,[23] today, it's over 55 percent—a dramatic shift.[24] There may not have been many metropolises in Jonah's world, but today, we have over 30 megacities with at least 10 million people, more than half of them in China and India. Tokyo (37 million), Delhi (32 million), and Shanghai (29 million) are the most populous. These cities have populations equivalent to sizable countries but relatively few churches or even individual Christian witnesses.

Jonah's Not-So-Hidden Message

Many books and sermons emphasize life lessons from the Book of Jonah, such as "Don't run from God," "We should obey," and "We need to be compassionate." Such character-building takeaways are certainly important, and Jonah's story includes many such lessons. But a real danger exists of missing the bigger point. Running from *what*? Obeying *what*? Compassionate toward *whom*? The Book of Jonah emphasizes the danger of failing to fulfill our mission as His people to be salt and light cross-culturally to the nations of the world.

Our time on earth is brief. This life is preparation for billions of years to come. Imagine arriving at the wedding feast of the Lamb described in Revelation 19, surrounded by saints from every people group on earth. Amidst the over-whelming joy and amazement, will we perhaps feel a tinge of regret? *Why didn't I realize this was the big picture? And why didn't I get more involved when I had the chance?*

In Romans 10:15, Paul writes, "How beautiful are the feet of those who bring good news!" He is borrowing language from passages like Isaiah 52:7, which describes messengers proclaiming the end of the Babylonian captivity to the people of Judah. We are called to be messengers with beautiful, well-traveled feet, overcoming every barrier to proclaim the good news of freedom from sin to people who have not heard it. Some of those people, like the Assyrians and the Sawi, may be part of violent cultures (after all, many cultures view America as violent, too). Their remote locations, complex languages and radically different worldviews may seem insurmountable obstacles.

We may sometimes wonder if some people can—or should—be saved. In the Book of Jonah, God thunders a resounding "Yes!" He is "not wanting anyone to perish, but everyone to come to repentance" (2 Peter 3:9). As His people, we should be praying regularly, "Lord, lead me to unexpected people and places. Give me Your compassion for people who seem far from Your grace."

Discussion Questions

1. Imagine God personally commanded you to preach in the streets of a megacity like Baghdad, Beijing, or Barcelona. How would you respond?
2. Have God's sovereignty and His intentions ever made you nervous?

3. When have you felt that God's mercy was unjust?
4. What categories of people do you think Christians are prone to consider (whether consciously or not) to be unworthy of God's grace?
5. What barriers to the spread of the gospel feel most challenging to you (e.g., geography, governments, other religions, number of cultures and languages, etc.)?

CHAPTER 3

An Unlikely Conscript

But Jonah ran away from the LORD and headed for Tarshish.
He went down to Joppa, where he found a ship bound for that
port. After paying the fare, he went aboard and sailed for Tarshish
to flee from the LORD. —Jonah 1:3

God's compassion for the Ninevites is surprising enough, but He was just getting started. He took it to another level by drafting Jonah for the task. We don't know a lot about Jonah. We don't even know if he wrote the book named for him or if he told his story to someone else who wrote it down. One thing we know for sure, though, is that he didn't want the job.

One might think that warning Nineveh of impending doom would have been much faster and easier if God had used an angel, a dream, or somebody besides Jonah. But He didn't. And He had His reasons. Have you ever noticed that when God intervenes in human affairs, He almost always uses people in the process?

Human Instruments for Divine Purposes

Jesus won the ultimate redemptive victory on the Cross, but ordinary human agency is a crucial dimension of God's plan. After all, the point of the Incarnation was for Jesus to become a man. Noah's ark didn't descend from heaven to miraculously save his family from the Flood. Noah had to build it. God promised Abraham, "I will bless all nations *through you.*" And when Jesus gave the Great Commission to a group of disciples, He said, "*You* go and make disciples among all nations."

To this day, God continues to work through human beings to accomplish His big plan. Jesus promises to be with us and to give us power for the task, but He doesn't bypass us to get the job done more efficiently. Our participation matters. Our words and actions are a primary means by which God is glorified. If we don't recognize that, our view of God's sovereignty can sometimes be misapplied to get us off the redemptive hook. "It's God's job to save the world," we might think. "I'm just going to live my life."

Strange as it may sound today, throughout much of history, many Christians viewed the Great Commission as applying only to the original apostles. Many believers assumed that the work of global gospel proclamation had been accomplished in the first century and was no longer relevant. According to some accounts, at a minister's meeting in Northampton in 1785, a young cobbler named William Carey was asked to suggest a topic for discussion. Carey had been studying the Bible and may have read *Voyage Round the World*, the tale of Captain James Cook's adventures in the Pacific. Hesitantly, Carey asked the gathered preachers, "Was not the command given to the Apostles, to teach all nations, obligatory on all succeeding ministers to the end of the world, seeing that the accompanying promise was of equal extent?"[25] A senior minister interrupted Carey. "Young man, sit down!" he said forcefully, "When God pleases to convert the heathen, he'll do it without consulting you or me."[26]

To suggest that "God is so great, He doesn't need us" can sound spiritual, and there's an element of truth to it. God accomplishes many things without our involvement, from the orbit of the planets to cellular reproduction in sea anemones. But it's worth asking, *How has our all-powerful God chosen to be glorified?* One important way is when His people, like the Lord Jesus Himself, complete the work He has given them to do (John 17:4, 18). It is more awesome, one could say, that God employs broken vessels like us than if He just did it Himself. God's love and patience are displayed as He works through Abraham's spiritual descendants to fulfill His ancient promise. He delights to see us grow into Christ-likeness as we pray, "Thy will be done," and then do His will.

A Hostile Witness

While Jonah was an unlikely messenger to Nineveh because of his resistance to the mission, he did have a few relevant qualifications on his resume. He was already a prophet who had spoken to the king of Israel. He had a reputation in his homeland. He recognized the voice of God. He had exhibited a degree of faithfulness in an increasingly godless culture. It's possible Jonah was one of the godliest people in the world at that time. Plus, he was strong-willed enough to take on a huge and dangerous challenge.

On the ship to Tarshish, Jonah told the sailors, "I am a Hebrew and I worship the LORD, the God of heaven, who made the sea and the dry land. ...[It] is my fault that this great storm has come upon you" (Jonah 1:9, 12). He had all the facts correct, but he still missed the point:

> He knows Yahweh is the creator and controller of nature (1:9), he knows he is in rebellion (1:12), he knows Yahweh is his only deliverance (2:2–10 [3–11]) and that Yahweh is gracious, compassionate, patient, and relenting (4:2). Jonah is the type of person who could pass any seminary theology test. But Jonah's actions demonstrate that knowing and submitting/trusting are two very different things. Jonah's orthodox theology is his downfall because he thinks he can control the when and the how of the theology—that he can control the God of his theology.[27]

As another scholar puts it, "The prophets were not mere machines; they had power to resist the will of God. However, this is the only instance on record where a prophet refused to carry out his commission."[28] That's quite a distinction.

I appreciate that Jonah is an open book. He may be wrong, but at least you know where he stands. And he's determined: "Jonah does not merely ignore or turn and walk away from Yahweh; he intentionally sets out to go in the opposite direction, and as far as he possibly can."[29] He sticks to his convictions through the rest of the story. But his strengths and self-certainty have a dark side. When God sends a tremendous storm on the open sea, "That he does not repent to Yahweh or even ask the sailors to take him back to dry land so he can fulfill his mission, let alone volunteer to jump, shows that his attitude and choices have not changed."[30]

Jonah's advice for the sailors to throw him overboard is

an acknowledgment of God's sovereign power, but it isn't yet repentance or obedience.

> He knows, now, that he cannot flee his responsibility, but that does not mean he will obey. ... Instead of addressing Yahweh, he addresses the sailors. By asking them to throw him overboard, he is seeking escape through their hands. Jonah's request for sailor-assisted suicide is not out of mercy for the sailors but out of a selfish desire to escape it all and die.[31]

While we can admire Jonah's forthrightness, he also elicits our pity. Here is a man who went "down" to Joppa (Jonah 1:3), *down* into the ship, *down* below deck (1:5), then *down* into the Mediterranean Sea (2:6) and eventually into the belly of a fish. Is it possible to sink any deeper?

During his three days inside the fish, Jonah does seem to humble himself and ask God for help. Quoting various Psalms (evidently knowing God's Word well), he cries out for mercy, vows sacrifices of praise to God, and testifies, "Salvation comes from the LORD" (Jonah 2:9). Scholars debate whether Jonah's response represents genuine repentance. Some read his prayer as a rather self-centered reflection, unlike David's prayer in Psalm 51. Jonah never explicitly admits that he was wrong to disobey God. However, I read Jonah's humility as genuine at the time. Whatever the case, after his traumatic experience and dramatic beach landing (the fish deserves some sympathy, too), Jonah's resentment of the Ninevites remains. Ethnocentrism dies hard. Jonah knows better than to disobey God a second time, but his attitude hasn't substantially improved.

Does this remind you of anyone? It's basically the story of Israel in the Old Testament, the record of a stubborn and uncooperative people. There are no surprises for God in Jonah's story. He chose someone He knew would be a challenge. Why would God entrust a message of compassion to so obstinate and unmerciful a messenger? I believe God chose Jonah for this assignment partly to illustrate His amazing sovereignty and grace. As outwardly righteous as Jonah may have been, he was still a product of his culture. He personified the willfulness and self-righteousness of his generation. Yet God had bound Himself by oath to fulfill His promise to Abraham. He would do so whether or not His servants chose to cooperate.

Ironically, even as Jonah fled from his assignment to preach to Gentiles, he ended up doing so anyway. And, at a practical level, Jonah's rebellion and flight might have played into God's strategy for shaking up Nineveh. Imagine Jonah arriving at the city gates with his skin bleached by the digestive juices of a giant fish, shouting about God's coming judgment on a city that worshipped a fish god (among others). No wonder he got their attention! Even in his rebellion and flight, he was playing into God's plan.

Yet another of God's purposes in choosing Jonah was to illustrate for Israel and hundreds of millions of people through the ages essential elements of His character and plans. What happened in Nineveh didn't stay in Nineveh. Jonah brought the story of his own disobedience and the Ninevites' repentance back home with him, much to Israel's shame. The Israelites were supposed to be a nation of priests who conveyed God's truth and blessing to the nations. They had failed in their role. A brash verbal processor was just the person to illustrate their condition. God uses different personalities for various roles in His great drama, all for His glory.

God's Habit of Choosing the Wrong Person

God's words to another prophet, Samuel, ring true through the ages: "People look at the outward appearance, but the LORD looks at the heart" (1 Samuel 16:7). Despite appearances, God's choices are always perfect and that includes His selection of imperfect people for noble tasks. We can be unlikely ministers of the gospel in all kinds of ways. Jonah's unwillingness makes him seem like a poor candidate. For some of us, it might be a lack of confidence, experience, health, finances, or skills. The barriers are real, just as Jonah's concerns were real. But God still wants the news of His surprising compassion to reach the far corners of the world. The fact that we don't appear well-suited at the moment need not keep us from playing a role in the divine drama. God is incredibly patient and loving as we learn and grow.

Throughout Scripture, we see examples of God choosing unlikely candidates for His work: Moses, the fugitive; Rahab, the prostitute; Gideon, the coward; David, the adulterer; Peter, the denier; and Paul, the persecutor. In more recent times, he has continued the practice. William Carey, the young cobbler chastised for asking about the relevance of the Great Commission, became known as the "father of modern missions." William Borden, an aristocrat from Illinois, gave his life for the gospel in Cairo at the age of 25. He was on his way to serve the Uyghur Muslim people of China. When he died in 1913 after a three-week battle with cerebral meningitis, he left the equivalent of $25 million to several mission organizations. Gladys Aylward, a diminutive London housemaid turned down by a mission agency, spent her life savings to buy a ticket on the Orient Express through a Russian warzone. Her service to orphans in China inspired the 1958 film *The Inn of the Sixth Happiness*.

And God is still using unlikely people today. As a boy, I had the privilege of meeting Elinor Young, a woman who made her way to the wilds of New Guinea as a missionary. She stood out in any setting because she was small in stature, wore leg braces, and used crutches. Elinor had contracted polio as a child. She also stood out to me because she was full of joy. She was called to be a missionary when a guest speaker visited her rural Washington town. She tells the story in her book *Running on Broken Legs*:

> The guest speaker was a man from China whose broken English indicated his origins and his physical appearance confirmed what he told us of severe malnutrition in his village during his childhood. His legs were bowed, his stomach protruded, and so did his teeth. He told us that living conditions in his village changed when missionaries brought the message of Jesus to them, and most of the villagers believed. They no longer needed to give large amounts of their food crops to the idols or profits from crops to buying opium, so they were better nourished.
>
> The speaker pled with our handful of farm families to see God's heartbeat for the people of the world who did not yet know Jesus. Then, of all things, he asked, "If anyone here feels God wants you to

be a missionary, would you step up to the front here and say so openly?" What a thing to ask of this audience of farm families. No one there could accept such an invitation. Except one. Me. I felt it was time to let my church family know what I knew in my heart. My stomach tightened, hoping the people there would understand.

I retrieved my crutches from under the pew in front of me and walked down the short aisle. As I did, I saw embarrassment in the eyes of the adults. I saw they were thinking, *Oh dear, this little girl doesn't know what she is doing.* I became embarrassed, knowing this looked like a foolish goal, and that made me look foolish.

Over thirty-five years later, Ormel, the only man who had been there that was not already in heaven, told me what happened after the service. He said that one of the men apologized to the speaker that the only person who had responded to his invitation was that "poor little crippled girl" who could never achieve such a goal.

As Ormel related this, he asked me, "You want to know what the speaker said to that?"

"Yes, please."

"That dear Chinese man said, 'Whom the Lord calls, he will use.'"[32]

God assigned Elinor an improbable task—sharing His love with the Kimyal people. That fierce tribe inhabited some of the highest and most rugged mountains of New Guinea. When Elinor arrived, the Kimyal, who were small in stature, marveled, "Look who the Creator has sent us!

A small lady just our size. And she has bad legs, just like some of us. He must love us very much!" Soon, Elinor learned the Kimyal language, shared the gospel, and began translating the Bible. Since she couldn't walk well with her braces, the new Kimyal believers carried her from village to village among the 13,000-foot peaks. They called her "Bad Legs" and announced everywhere they went, "Bad Legs has brought a good message!"

Elinor Young exemplifies God's unmatched ability to use any of us. She served among the Kimyal for 18 years. One of the most inspiring videos you can watch on YouTube is "Indonesia's Kimyal People Welcome the New Testament."[33] You can also find a short film about Elinor's story, appropriately called "Bad Legs."[34] It's worth showing to your children or grandchildren. The bottom line? Fruitful messengers are not always the obvious ones.

You've Been Chosen, Too

We may not be as aware of it as Elinor Young, but we all have "bad legs." We're all imperfect vessels. It could be that those legs are the very things God wants to use for His glory. If, like Jonah, what's holding you back is a faulty perspective about God and the people He loves, I suggest yielding more readily than Jonah did. And if you can't muster your heart to follow God in what He may be calling you to do, you can pray with me, "Lord, please take away ideas and desires that are not from You and replace them with Yours."

Jonah was called to an overwhelming task—persuading more than 100,000 people in a foreign country to repent and change their lifestyle! We can feel overwhelmed as well.

About eight billion people live in the world today. If we all stood in a line, taking up a foot of space each, that line of precious souls would stretch to the moon and back almost three times. It's impossible for us to truly comprehend such numbers. Think of driving coast-to-coast across the U.S., with men, women, and children lined up on the side of the freeway for all 2,800 miles. That's barely scratching the surface of how many people exist on Earth today. You'd have to drive that cross-country route about 500 times to glimpse each person even once. Most of them do not know Jesus as their Savior. More than half of them do not even know a Christian.[35]

Not only do we have a lot of people to reach, but they also comprise many people groups, each with a unique language, culture, history, and worldview. Of the 17,000 people groups in the world today, about 7,000 still have almost no access to the gospel.[36] About a quarter of the earth's population are born and die without ever hearing, much less understanding, God's offer of salvation.[37] That is overwhelming on an even bigger scale than what Jonah faced.

Nevertheless, amid vast opportunity and need, God continues to use unlikely people to bless the nations. He has a wide cast of characters for His divine drama, and there's a place for you to play a part. Remember, God doesn't limit Himself to volunteers. He didn't ask Jonah if he wanted to go to Nineveh. He didn't ask the disciples if they'd like to make disciples of all nations. And He didn't ask Paul if he felt inspired to take the gospel to the non-Jewish world.

The key to the impact of God's people isn't their skills or evident qualifications, as helpful as they may prove to be.

More fundamentally, it boils down to the question Jesus asked Peter repeatedly over breakfast on the shore of the Sea of Galilee, "Do you love Me?" (John 21:15-17). As we fall more in love with Jesus, we become like Him and share His passion for a lost world. Our instructions may not be as clear as Jonah's, but God is just as much in control of our path.

Are you willing to trust God for new roles or responsibilities that seem scary? Will you take some steps toward those who have little or no access to the gospel? It can make a big difference in your life trajectory, whether or not you ever move to a far corner of the world. Over the centuries, millions of Christians have contributed to the fulfillment of the Great Commission in a huge variety of ways. So don't get overwhelmed by the task; if you do, keep moving anyway. I love the saying, "Courage is fear that has said its prayers." The spiritual needs of the world are vast. Let's pray anyway, "Lord, raise up your chosen instruments!"

Discussion Questions

1. What are some examples of times God used you to do something instead of acting directly Himself?
2. This chapter describes Jonah as qualified but unwilling for his assignment. What about you? Is your involvement in global missions limited by your skills? Experience? Motivation? Or something else?
3. What makes you an unlikely minister of the gospel? What examples from the chapter resonated with you? (e.g., Moses, the fugitive; Rahab, the prostitute; Gideon, the coward; David, the adulterer; Peter, the denier; Paul, the persecutor; William Carey, the cobbler; William

Borden, the aristocrat; Gladys Aylward, the maid; Elinor Young, the polio survivor)

4. Are you willing for God to use your "bad legs" for His glory?

5. What steps can you take this week toward those with little or no access to the gospel?

CHAPTER 4

An Extraordinary Response

Then they cried out to the LORD, "Please, LORD, do not let us die for taking this man's life. Do not hold us accountable for killing an innocent man, for you, LORD, have done as you pleased." Then they took Jonah and threw him overboard, and the raging sea grew calm. At this the men greatly feared the LORD, and they offered a sacrifice to the LORD and made vows to him. —Jonah 1:14-16

We have seen God's compassionate plan to prevent Nineveh's destruction, His peculiar choice of an envoy, and Jonah's staunch resistance to the assignment. The conscripted prophet wants no part in sparing such an evil city and tries to sabotage God's plan by fleeing. How will God respond to such blatant insubordination?

Going West, Young Man?

At first, God seems to bide His time. I picture Jonah plotting his escape over a period of sleepless nights. He sells his townhouse, cashes in his savings, hugs his sweetheart goodbye, and hikes several days down to Joppa. There, he negotiates an affordable fare on a decent-looking ship bound for Tarshish, the westernmost extremity of the world as he knows it. So far, so good. Once the boat is out in the middle of the Mediterranean, though, God's wind begins to blow (Jonah 1:4).

Maybe Jonah, exhausted from his journey and the emotional toll of leaving his loved ones and homeland, finds himself increasingly seasick. After all, running from God can be draining. So, he burrows himself away in the belly of the boat and falls into a deep sleep. As he sleeps, God sends a great wind. Storms invariably follow disobedience. They are both a consequence of sin and a warning signal to change directions. Violating God's design can seem tempting and painless for a season but always leads to trouble.

In Jonah's story, a literal storm rages, and the crew becomes truly alarmed. Conditions deteriorate to the point where they hurl valuable cargo overboard. Jonah's disobedience costs not only him but everyone else, too. The hull of the ship groans and threatens to splinter under the strain. In their fear and desperation, the sailors call out for divine help. The trouble is, quite a few gods are represented among the Gentile crew. Which god has been angered? Zeus? Baal? Melqart? Unfortunately, the person who should be pointing the way to the true God is fast asleep. Everyone's lives are in mortal danger, but Jonah remains oblivious.

The sailors each instinctively call out to their own gods for help (Jonah 1:5), but nothing seems to work. Then someone shouts above the storm, "There's one more guy down below!" The captain descends and shakes Jonah awake. "How can you sleep? Get up and call on your god!" Think about that for a minute. The pagan captain of the ship is commanding

Israel's prophet to wake up and pray for sinners who are under the judgment of God. It's all completely backward!

A Salty Conversation

As we've noted, every word in the Book of Jonah is carefully chosen. The famous fish is mentioned in only three verses of the book (1:17; 2:1, 10), but Jonah's interactions with the sailors dominate almost the entire first chapter. Clearly, their presence was important to the writer and the Holy Spirit.

The sailors' prominence is even more surprising if you consider that Jonah wasn't even "supposed" to meet them. He never would have been on that boat if he had set off promptly for Nineveh. We find that even in Jonah's disobedience, God's purposes prevail. In this case, God takes the opportunity to introduce Himself to a group of pagans. And these aren't just any pagans. These are sailors—perhaps among the crustiest of pagans. In a brilliant move, God arranges for Jonah's discipline to double as an evangelistic opportunity.

The sailors are clearly spiritually minded people. They represent cultures in which many of the right questions about man's relationship with the divine are met with many wrong answers. As Jonah rubs the sleep from his eyes, the crew devises a way for the gods to divulge who is responsible for the calamity of the storm. They cast lots, and sure enough, it falls to Jonah.

Once Jonah is identified as the culprit, they inundate him with questions. "Why is this happening? Who are you? Where do you come from?" and finally, "What should we do to make things right with your god?" The sailors present quite a contrast with Jonah. They are thoughtful and considerate, and they pray when Jonah doesn't. While he sleeps, they are alert. They seem more interested and responsive to Jonah's God than he is. Jonah tells them he is running away from the true God who made the ocean they're sailing on. They immediately believe him and are horrified (Jonah 1:9-10). In some ways, "These heathen mariners were more aroused and alarmed by the flagrant disobedience of Jonah than the prophet of God himself was. What a rebuke it should have been to him!"[38]

Role Reversal

Having understood their plight, the crew must decide what to do. They are willing to risk their lives to spare Jonah's, even though he has knowingly jeopardized them and cost them their livelihood (the cargo thrown overboard in verse 5). Here is another note of irony. Jonah has endangered the sailors, which mirrors Assyria's threat to Israel. But unlike Jonah, the sailors respond with compassion. No matter how hard the storm rages, Jonah apparently does not attempt to set things right with God. We don't see him repent, pray for the ship's safety, or promise to go to Nineveh at the first opportunity. He believes that God is merciful, but he doesn't ask for mercy on the ship—for himself or the unwitting accomplices who are being punished for his disobedience.

The crew, on the other hand, tries to row back to shore, likely to send Jonah off to Nineveh to appease his God. Typically, ships were kept out at sea during storms to avoid being driven onto rocks in shallow water.[39] In the end, the sailors realize they have no choice. They must throw Jonah to a seemingly certain death or perish themselves. But first, they cry out to God not to judge them as murderers (Jonah 1:14). If Jonah had been interested in saving the sailors and was convinced that his death was the only way, one would think he could have jumped in himself rather than making them throw him overboard against their consciences.[40]

Throughout the story, the sailors act appropriately based on every piece of information they receive. When the sea calms as soon as the prophet disappears into the depths, we are told the crew "greatly feared the LORD, and they offered a sacrifice to the LORD and made vows to him" (Jonah 1:16). We can't be sure if all of them respond with genuine saving faith, but they definitely respond! Israel's great God has shown them great mercy, even though Jonah never asked Him to. The unbelieving crew members show greater spiritual insight and better behavior than the prophet. For Israelites of Jonah's time, this should have been a humbling story to tell.

A Spectacular Surrender

As Jonah blinks in the sunlight on the rocky coastline of Libya (or wherever the fish spit him up), he gets the dreaded call again. God still wants him to preach in Assyria. This time, he obeys. Try to picture Jonah finally trudging miserably into the megacity of Nineveh. He might be recognizable as a citizen of Israel, a country that Assyria has already attacked at least once. He probably looks like he's weathered some tough times.

Jonah begins to call out to the crowds of men, women, and children who are gawking at him, "Forty more days and Nineveh will be overthrown" (Jonah 3:4). I would expect a society known for cruelty and violence to laugh in his face, ignore him, or throw him off the city wall. After all, Jonah comes from a subject colony of the empire and he is conveying a treasonous message. Instead, they respond with alarm and a strong dose of humility. In another remarkable twist in the story, the Ninevites immediately believe Jonah's message. Here's how the Bible describes it:

> Jonah began by going a day's journey into the city, proclaiming, "Forty more days and Nineveh will be overthrown." The Ninevites believed God. A fast was proclaimed, and all of them, from the greatest to the least, put on sackcloth.
>
> When Jonah's warning reached the king of Nineveh, he rose from his throne, took off his royal robes, covered himself with sackcloth and sat down in the dust. This is the proclamation he issued in Nineveh (Jonah 3:4-10):
>
> "By the decree of the king and his nobles:
>
> Do not let people or animals, herds or flocks, taste anything; do not let them eat or drink. But let people and animals be covered with sackcloth. Let everyone call urgently on God. Let them give up their evil ways and their violence. Who knows? God may yet relent and with compassion turn from his fierce anger so that we will not perish."
>
> When God saw what they did and how they turned from their evil ways, he relented and did not bring on them the destruction he had threatened.

It's important to note that Jonah's message is primarily about impending disaster. He doesn't sugar-coat the future.

Good news is only good to the degree that it contrasts with an alternative. I wonder sometimes if, in our proclamation of the gospel, we don't adequately clarify the alternative. Whereas Jonah emphasizes the bad news and perhaps even focuses exclusively on it, in our day, we often make the opposite mistake. We may describe the situation as, "You're okay, but you could be even better off with Jesus." The reality is unbelievers are *not* okay.

We don't know what else Jonah may have said to the Ninevites. We know it was a message that God gave him (Jonah 3:2). Maybe he told them his story and admitted, "I disobeyed God and look what happened to me. I suggest you not do the same!" Whatever the case, the Ninevites responded by literally begging for mercy. The whole city repented in sackcloth, from the king on his throne to the cows in the field. They did the opposite of what Israel and its king were doing.

Sometimes, we glide over this episode because we know it so well, but the Assyrian response is staggering. The biblical record spends a lot of time on Nineveh's repentance, which shows that it's another major focus of the book. Some scholars suggest the people may have been primed for the message by a series of plagues or floods and a total solar eclipse just before Jonah arrived.[41] Others think they had experienced some military and territorial setbacks. Yet others point out that the Assyrians worshipped the fish god Dagon, among other gods, and might have connected that with Jonah's big fish story.[42] But whatever additional factors God may or may not have used, the speed and intensity of the Ninevites' response remain astonishing:

The sacred record preserves for us only five words
of Jonah's message (in the original of 3:4), but it
was one of the greatest messages ever preached by
man, if not the greatest. Nowhere do we read in
the Bible or outside of it that one message from
a servant of God was used of God to so great an
extent. For the whole city of Nineveh believed
God! Nothing remotely approximating this has
ever taken place in the history of revivals. Jonah
was a sign, but the people did not concern themselves with the prophet. They believed God.[43]

Word of Jonah's arrival and message spreads quickly,
reaching even the king. The king immediately rises from his
throne, changes into beggar's clothing, and sits in the dusty
street. His powerful nobles join him in showing unbridled
contrition. Everyone fasts, dons uncomfortable sackcloth
clothing, and sits in the dirt. A law is quickly passed requiring
everyone to go without food or drink. All violence and immorality are outlawed. Instead of eating and drinking and carrying
on business, everyone, without exception, is to pray. No sector
of society is exempt. Even the livestock are deprived of food
and water. The Ninevites utterly humble themselves, hoping
that the God of Israel will relent from His fierce anger. If I
had to choose one word from the text to summarize Nineveh's
response, it would be "urgently" (Jonah 3:8).

As with the sailors, scholars disagree whether the Ninevites'
response to Jonah's warning demonstrated genuine saving
faith. Jesus later implies their repentance was real (Matthew
12:41). Even if their contrition is only fear-inspired and relatively short-lived, it is still astounding in its intensity. The

prophet Nahum's scathing rebuke will eventually be fulfilled, and Assyria will be destroyed as Jonah hoped, but God postpones their destruction by almost a century.[44] No national repentance on this scale has ever been seen in Israel.

A World Prepared

The repentance of the people of Nineveh is truly amazing. The Ninevites have very little knowledge of the God of Israel, but they take a chance that He might, perhaps, be merciful. Jonah knows for certain that He is merciful, and he resents it. The contrast couldn't be greater. Jonah experiences miraculous salvation despite his sin but is not ready to extend that same grace to the Ninevites.[45]

An important thread in the Book of Jonah involves the repentance of those from whom we would least expect it. The unreached world is much riper and more responsive than many Christians think. God said as much to the prophet Ezekiel:

> You are not being sent to a people of obscure speech and strange language, but to the people of Israel—not to many peoples of obscure speech and strange language, whose words you cannot understand. *Surely if I had sent you to them, they would have listened to you.* But the people of Israel are not willing to listen to you because they are not willing to listen to me, for all the Israelites are hardened and obstinate (Ezekiel 3:5-7, emphasis added).

Jesus warned the unrepentant people of Capernaum, "If the miracles that were performed in you had been performed in Sodom, it would have remained to this day" (Matthew

11:23). Pause to think about that for a moment. Could there be any stronger rebuke? The Scriptures give many other examples of the surprising responsiveness of unlikely people. Some of the first people to worship Jesus after His birth were foreigners, Magi from a distant land (Matthew 2:1-2). Jesus complimented the "great faith" of the Canaanite woman (Matthew 15:28).

During Jesus' time on earth, centurions represented the Roman Empire's ruthless, colonialist regime. I would expect them to care very little about the teachings of a Jewish rabbi. And yet, it was a centurion of whom Jesus said, "I have not found anyone in Israel with such great faith" (Matthew 8:10). And it was a centurion who acknowledged at the Cross, "Surely he was the Son of God!" (Matthew 27:54). In fact, every time Jesus commends someone for their faith in the Gospels, it is a Gentile. The apostle Paul's last recorded words in Acts are, "Therefore I want you to know that God's salvation has been sent to the Gentiles, and they will listen!" (Acts 28:28).

Jesus often taught and demonstrated that He had come to call Samaritans, prostitutes, and other "undesirables" from the outskirts of society (Luke 14:21-23). He refers to them as His "other sheep" (John 10:16). The religious leaders of Israel were generally the least receptive to the principles of the kingdom of heaven that Jesus taught, even though a few of them did believe. The important point here isn't about Jews and Gentiles. It's about the contrast between those who have access to the truth yet hoard or reject it and those who've never had the option but are ready to respond.

The Book of Jonah stands as a rebuke to God's people who have the light of truth. I suspect there's a lesson here for us as well. I have observed that many Western Christians think, at least subconsciously, that it's harder to reach people of other religions, be they Muslims, Hindus, Buddhists, or animists in faraway places, than people in our own familiar society. I don't think that's necessarily true. God has prepared people everywhere to receive the good news of salvation. Many times, we come across them in unexpected places. And in many cases, those with the least access to the gospel are the most receptive once they hear and understand its message.

A Fortuitous Encounter

Some years ago, I joined several thousand evangelical Christian leaders from around the world in Cape Town, South Africa, for a major conference on world evangelization. During the opening session, we were warned to be cautious walking the streets, especially after dark. One evening, as the sun was setting, I set off to walk the 20 minutes to my hotel. Suddenly, out of the shadows, a strong young African man materialized at my side. He was muttering something that I couldn't immediately understand. Finally, I realized he was saying, "Give me your money!" He now had my full attention. I looked down and saw him pointing a switchblade at my side, blocking it with his jacket so others couldn't see it as we walked along.

I don't know exactly what came over me at that moment, but without thinking, I responded as I would to any stranger who asked me for money. "I might give you some," I told him, "but I'd like to get to know you first." Now, it was his turn to be caught off guard! I pressed my advantage, asking about his situation. He explained that he had been released from prison three days earlier and was hungry.

"Have you ever heard about Jesus?" I asked.

"Oh yeah, I used to live with my grandmother, and she made me go to church. I know about Jesus."

"Did your grandmother pray for you?"

"Yes," he said.

I went on, "God is answering your grandmother's prayers today. You pulled your knife on me, hoping to get a little money, but God has something bigger in mind. He sent me to tell you that He loves you."

He eventually folded the knife back into his pocket as we walked on. When we arrived at my hotel, we stood under a streetlight and prayed. My would-be robber asked God to forgive him. Then I gave him a little cash and told him, "Get yourself a meal, but more importantly, look for a church. Tell them your situation and ask for help. God has given you much more tonight than you asked for." We hugged, and he disappeared into the night.

That was a 15-minute appointment that only God could have arranged. To me, it was a lesson in being alert to the metaphorical sailors and Ninevites all around us. There I was, at a big, strategic conference focused on world evangelism, and maybe the most spiritually significant thing I did that day was get mugged on the way home.

Being salt and light in our world—the whole world—is not only about strategies and methods and statistics. It's also about the individuals we encounter along the way. Who has God brought into your life so you can share His word of blessing? Who do you assume to be in the "resistant" category who may, in fact, be surprisingly open to the message of hope and deliverance in Jesus? May our planned strategies leave room for "chance" encounters so that the description of Antioch in Pisidia will fit us as well, "All who were appointed for eternal life believed" (Acts 13:48).

Eternity in Their Hearts

God has prepared modern-day sailors and Ninevites all over the world. Clusters of people in unexpected places are ready to respond to His message. I find that motivating. No matter where we go in the world, some segment of the population will eventually be responsive to the gospel. In Jonah's case, a whole city repented. We aren't promised results on the same scale, but we should anticipate and watch for what God may want to do through us. Often, God uses the splendor of creation, catastrophes, and social dislocation to soften people's hearts, alert them to the fundamental questions of life, and draw them to Himself. Don't assume that anyone, or any community, is beyond the gospel's reach. Instead, let's give them an opportunity to respond to the truth, one way or another.

My father, Don Richardson, unpacks the concept of redemptive analogies in his book *Eternity in Their Hearts*.[46] Redemptive analogies are historical and cultural "keys" that God has implanted in the belief systems of people around the world. They come in various forms—legends, names for a Supreme God, unique customs, linguistic features, and other eye-openers that bear testimony to God's care for those communities. When gospel-bearers finally arrive, sometimes people ask, "Where have you been all these centuries?"

Now, that doesn't mean we won't also be met with strong opposition. Jesus, Paul, and others found both receptive and hostile people wherever they went. When we proclaim God's message clearly, interested listeners usually identify them-selves. Opponents do, too.

In any situation, we don't know whether God is preparing a few or a multitude. We also don't know His timing. Our gospel efforts could sow seeds that won't germinate for years or even generations. Scientist Jane Shen-Miller holds a world record for successfully germinating 1,000-year-old seeds.[47]

In Korea, hundreds of missionaries gave their lives in what seemed for almost a century to be a wasted effort. The small, persecuted Korean church they established sent its first missionaries in 1974. Just 40 years later, more than 27,000 Korean missionaries were serving in 170 countries.[48] Their impact on world missions is impossible to quantify. The efforts of those first generations of missionaries weren't wasted after all, but the fruit was hidden until God chose to reveal it.

We may not immediately see results when we go into the world to share the gospel. But take heart. We don't just have hope of an eventual response. We have a promise from God and a proven record. Church history is full of examples like what happened in Korea.

I'm thankful that when Jesus talked about the harvest around the world, He used the descriptor "ripe" (John 4:35), Which is as true today as ever. Jesus told His followers, "The harvest is plentiful, but the workers are few. Ask the Lord of the harvest, therefore, to send out workers into his harvest field" (Matthew 9:37-38). The main challenge in Jesus' mind was not the unresponsiveness of the unevangelized but the scarcity of laborers. And this scarcity can be traced to a corresponding lack of perspective and urgency among God's people. It's a Jonah problem. We can be part of the answer to our own prayers for laborers, asking, "Lord, lead me to those you've prepared."

Discussion Questions

1. When have you been surprised by an unbeliever's spiritual openness?
2. What might Nineveh-level repentance look like in your town or city?
3. Who has God brought into your life so you can share His word of blessing?
4. How can you remind yourself to be on the lookout for metaphorical sailors and Ninevites this week?
5. Take a minute to scroll through today's world news headlines. How might God's promise and track record of building His Church all over the world (as He has in Korea) influence the way you pray about current events?

CHAPTER 5

A Merciless Missionary

Those who cling to worthless idols
turn away from God's love for them.
But I, with shouts of grateful praise,
will sacrifice to you.
What I have vowed I will make good.
I will say, "Salvation comes from the LORD."
—Jonah 2:8-9

Imagine for a moment that your church has sent a new missionary to Pyongyang, Tehran, or some other major urban center that feels dangerous and inhospitable to you. You're excited for him, but you know it will be challenging to communicate the gospel in an unfamiliar culture. You might wonder if he'll make it very long in such an intense ministry context. Your doubts are further fueled by an awareness that he's questioned God's judgment in the past and exhibited, let's say, an independent spirit.

Now imagine that in this missionary's first newsletter from the field, he announces that the entire city has turned to Christ. A public fast has been declared, and throngs line the streets, crying out for God's mercy. Even the Supreme Leader or Ayatollah has gone on television to confess his sins and call his people to repentance. It all happened in response to a brief sermon that your missionary preached. You might be a little skeptical. But assuming you verified it was true, what would you expect him to do next? Go on a speaking tour? Write a book on keys to effective evangelism? Take early retirement? Our biblical protagonist finds himself in such a situation. His next move is to hunker down in a lean-to in the desert east of the city.

Here's the last big surprise of the book: it's not just the Ninevites who need heart change. Despite all he's been through, Jonah still needs it, too.

A Desperate Prayer

In the final chapter of the Book of Jonah, God goes to work on His prophet once again. Remember, this isn't Jonah's first time in the spiritual ICU. Let's review what happened the first time, back in chapter 2. We could call it Jonah's "darkness retreat" at the Big Fish Lodge.

I only recently heard of a darkness retreat. The idea seems to have caught on when Green Bay Packers quarterback Aaron Rodgers spent four days in complete isolation in an Oregon cabin specifically designed for sensory deprivation. He wanted to contemplate his future without distractions. For as little as $250 per night, you can apparently sit in a completely dark room, alone with your thoughts. The walls are painted dark blue or black to absorb any stray rays of light. Meals are delivered through a light-proof food box. No phones, noises, or other distractions. It's just an utterly dark cabin deep in a snowy forest. The goal, they say, is to become more present.

To clear away the mental cobwebs and get back in touch with who you really are.[49]

Can you imagine it? Now, suppose you're in complete darkness but not in a comfortable room with plenty of air and a bed to stretch out on. Instead, you've been thrown into a raging sea and swallowed by a big fish. Instead of being served seafood, you've become seafood. You're gasping for air in the pulsating intestinal cavity of a massive creature. For three days, you're barely able to move. You are wet, cold, and dehydrated. Gastric juices are dissolving your skin. And if you were seasick on the ship, imagine how you're feeling now!

Nineveh may have meant something like "a house for fish."[50] Jonah refused to go to Nineveh, so now, in a stroke of divine irony, he has a fish for his "house." Amid the importance of what's at stake here, I can see hints of God's humor and awesome power. Resisting Him is foolish and futile. Jonah is contending with the creator of galaxies, the "God of heaven, who made the sea and the dry land" (Jonah 1:9). Jonah has described this God, with overtones of national pride, to non-Jewish sailors. Now, he is experiencing God's tremendous disciplinary power. Remember, this isn't just an allegory. It happened.

Jonah's underwater darkness retreat is strong medicine. In one of many expressions of irony, a man who thus far has been disinclined to ask for God's help, whether for himself or others, is finally driven to his knees. Jonah belatedly does what the pagan sailors much more readily did and begged him to do (Jonah 1:6, 14). He "calls out" to his God. He has bottomed out, going down "deep in the realm of the dead," engulfed in waves, suffocating in seaweed, feeling "banished from [God's] sight" (Jonah 2:2, 4). Words fail to describe the severity of his predicament adequately.

Jonah has to be brought to the end of himself before he comes to grips with reality. Often, we learn life's greatest lessons in the most painful of circumstances. From inside the belly of the fish, Jonah turns to prayer. A full eight verses of the 48 verses of the book are devoted to his cry of desperation.

Calling out to God is one of the themes of the Book of Jonah. Jonah's prayer of repentance provides the center spine. Jonah's prayer employs a chiastic structure that emphasizes the importance and beauty of the core message: "Salvation comes from the LORD" (Jonah 2:9). Some have even argued that this is, in fact, the *central thought of the whole Bible*. A prayer that begins in desperation concludes with a song of thanksgiving. Structurally, and through wordplay and a pivot from narrative to poetry (a Hebrew technique for emphasis), the book's main message and the central role of prayer are highlighted. Jonah finally acknowledges God's *hesed*—His steadfast love. For the moment, at least, Jonah recognizes and appreciates God's nature.

Prayer is a feature of true humility and repentance. We acknowledge His sovereignty and superiority when we call out to God for mercy. We recognize that we are wrong and can't fix things. We catch a glimpse of reality—of God as He is and ourselves in our true condition. We recognize that we are helpless before Him and without Him. We finally look to God's temple, the place of His presence and power. That's what Israel refused to do, and Jonah, in his pride, wasn't willing to do it despite his privileged role as God's spokesperson.

Whereas the sailors and the Ninevites readily prayed, confessed, sacrificed and made vows, Jonah only called out to God as a last resort. This revealing sequence happens in both halves of the Jonah narrative, giving us insight into the fundamental condition of Jonah's heart. Only when he spends time in the most humiliating and restrictive circumstances does Jonah awaken to the realities of who he is in relation to God and His mission.

A Smashing Success

Fast-forwarding once again to Nineveh, Jonah has hit a home run. More accurately, God has been remarkably merciful once again despite His messenger's inadequacies. Indeed, "Salvation comes from the LORD" (Jonah 2:9).

If I were the one writing the Book of Jonah, I think I would have wrapped it up after chapter 3. That's the logical, positive "Hallmark Channel" ending. Sure, Jonah disobeyed at first, but some quality time "down under" set him straight. He survived three days inside a fish and walked hundreds of miles through enemy territory. He preached in the imposing metropolis of a hostile empire. As a direct result of his ministry, well over 100,000 idolatrous people, led by the king himself, put on sackcloth, fasted, and pleaded for God's mercy. Such a societal shift has never been seen before. Even the livestock joined in. Jonah is now a wildly successful prophet. He's learned his lesson. There's so much to celebrate!

But, strangely, there's more to the story.

Chapter 4 should describe the follow-up to Nineveh's repentance. Talk about a need for discipleship! Jonah is probably one of the most effective missionaries who has ever lived. If he were committed to helping the Assyrians learn to worship and obey Yahweh, Israel's true God, he would surely be extremely busy. Jonah should have been cheering the Ninevites on and teaching them the marvelous theological truths that God had recently reinforced in his own life:

1. Who God is: "The God of heaven, who made the sea and the dry land" (Jonah 1:9).
2. What true worship looks like: "Those who cling to idols turn away from God's love for them" (Jonah 2:8).
3. God's offer of amnesty: "A gracious and compassionate God, slow to anger and abounding in love, a God who relents from sending calamity" (Jonah 4:2).

But no. Instead, we find Jonah sulking on a hillside outside the city.

The Book of Jonah doesn't end with the celebration we expect because, as we've noted since the beginning, this story isn't just about the salvation of Nineveh. It has "a yet greater climax, the true goal and objective of the whole book. Because God must teach His servant (and us through him) certain truths about the narrowness of his heart and the boundless greatness of God's own blessed heart."[51] The closing chapter emphasizes how much Jonah still has to learn, even after God has used him remarkably.

The Slow Learner

In the Bible, a 40-day period is mentioned at least ten times. It consistently signifies a period of testing and spiritual challenge. At some point during or after the 40-day warning period, Jonah realizes that God isn't going to destroy Nineveh, and his pent-up frustration erupts. While this has been a time of testing for Nineveh, it has also been a test for Jonah, and he fails. Any remorse he may have shown in the fish has evaporated in the desert heat, and he is back to his cantankerous, self-centered default settings. Established attitudes and worldviews die hard. Jonah may have learned to cooperate with God outwardly when necessary for survival, but his heart still isn't in it. Being with the Ninevites has reinforced his disdain for them and their culture. Despite his preaching to others, it appears that Jonah does not yet grasp, or at least doesn't appreciate at an emotional level, God's compassion and loving plan for the 99.9 percent of the world that is not Jewish.

Jonah is so disappointed at Nineveh's forgiveness that he lashes out at God, "I knew all along You were going to do this! See, I was justified in heading for Tarshish. I knew You were too gracious to destroy Nineveh like You said. These horrible people manipulated You and took advantage of Your softness. I don't want to live in such an unfair world. Just kill me like You almost did before!" It's as if Jonah is saying, "The more I know You, the less I like You!"

And God agrees with him, "Yes, you're right. This was my intention from the beginning. I wanted to have mercy on this great city." God is an emotional being, too. Much as Jesus would one day grieve over Jerusalem, so God grieves over the great city of Nineveh, shrouded in spiritual darkness. Its people can't even "tell their right hand from their left" (Jonah 4:11). They've lost sight of the difference between right and wrong. As a result, Nineveh is on a collision course with disaster. God called Jonah to be His instrument of correction and mercy, only to find Himself with an even bigger challenge. His chosen servant is more belligerent than the crusty sailors or the violent Ninevites. It seems they weren't the only ones who had idols—values that encroached on God's rightful place in their hearts. Jonah had his own as well. And they were well entrenched.

Have you ever been terribly wronged by someone? Perhaps they've done something to you that permanently altered your life, and they can never compensate you for it. Once resentment and unforgiveness take root, they can be hard to give up. If you were to forgive the offender, you would give up the psychological leverage you feel you deserve. You would release them from their debt to you. Releasing such a person, much less welcoming them into your life, is very hard to do. But it's a key to true freedom.

For the second time in the book, Jonah has been driven to prayer, but it's not a prayer of repentance. Instead, it's a prayer of resentment. Jonah is so angry that he talks in suicidal terms (Jonah 4:3). God's mercy is driving him mad. This time, though, rather than incarcerating Jonah inside an animal, God takes a gentler but still firm approach. He understands that the core of Jonah's issue is self-centeredness. The Lord responds with a penetrating question, "Is it right for you to be angry?" (Jonah 4:4).

Jonah, having been commissioned a second time at the beginning of chapter 3, is now in the midst of a heart procedure that takes place over, at least symbolically, three key days. The first day, he walked into the "house for fish." He preached a message of coming judgment, and the city repented in short order. Then he went east of the city and sat down under his makeshift shelter (Jonah 4:5). It was the second time he relaxed by himself when people nearby were in danger.

Now, on the second key day, God gives Jonah a real-life object lesson. He provides a leafy plant to shade him from the Middle Eastern sun (Jonah 4:6). This makes Jonah very happy. I can testify that Iraq in the summer can be unbearably hot! Jonah spends the day patiently awaiting the destruction of Nineveh. On the third day, God provides a worm and a blazing hot sun (Jonah 4:7). Jonah, feeling entitled, makes it known that he is not pleased. While God grieves over a lost world, Jonah grieves over his lost shade. Day three is a very hot, very bad day.

Next, God follows up with a second round of inquiry, "Is it right for you to be angry about the plant?" (Jonah 4:9). Jonah declares he has every right to be angry and even has the right to die—the right to remove himself from God's sanctifying process and plan. Like his nation, Jonah doesn't really understand God's grace or the scale of His loving, global heart. The book concludes with a question that cuts through all the clutter and echoes through the halls of redemptive history: "Should I not have concern for the great city of Nineveh?" (Jonah 4:11).

Thankfully, unlike Jonah, you and I are much easier for God to work with, right? We don't have our own self-serving lesser agendas like this renegade prophet, do we?

God is an amazing multi-tasker. Throughout this story, He has demonstrated His compassion for Nineveh and simultaneously taken Jonah on a journey of personal growth. God first blessed Jonah with an extraordinary privilege and responsibility, "Go and take my message of warning to one of the greatest cities in the world." When Jonah rebelled, God didn't destroy him. Instead, He "sent" a great wind (Jonah 1:4). Then He "provided" a great fish to swallow him just as he was about to drown (Jonah 1:17). God "commanded" the fish to vomit Jonah onto dry land (Jonah 2:10). Then He apparently blessed Jonah with recovered health and strength for the long journey. He protected him from the Assyrians and produced miraculous spiritual fruit. One thing is clear: God loves Jonah. The missing factor is Jonah's love for God.

I am amazed at God's grace in dealing with Jonah at this late stage of the story. God could easily have decommissioned him or consigned him to another fishy purgatory. Instead, He kept working with him. God is so patient with us!

An Unsatisfying Ending

The book closes with God's words of correction to Jonah. He says, in essence, "If you feel this bitter over the death of a plant that shaded you for a short time, how do you think I feel about the destiny of thousands of people whom I created in My image and daily sustain?" And with that, the story is over. It feels abrupt to us, but the Holy Spirit ends the story this way on purpose. The reader is left in the position of Jonah, pondering God's provocative question.

I hope Jonah repented and went home to preach to Israel about God's compassion for the least deserving. But it's possible he clung to his bitterness. Someone else could have heard his self-righteous version of the story, recognized the profound truths about God's compassion for the lost, and written it down as a testimony to future generations. Regardless of whether Jonah allowed himself to be transformed by the events of the book, God's main points are crystal clear by the end of chapter 4:

> (a) He is gracious toward all nations, toward Gentiles as well as Israelites; (b) He is sovereign; (c) He punishes rebellions; and (d) He wants His own people to obey Him, to be rid of religious sham, and to place no limits on His universal love and grace.[52]

I would add one more thought: *God wants His people to be like Him and fulfill their mission of compassionately representing Him to a lost world.*

Jonah isn't the hero of this story. God is. Despite His prophet's efforts to the contrary, God saved the sailors, Jonah, and Nineveh. His unstoppable love was displayed for all to see, including us, thousands of years later. And we can each choose our response to God's final question. Should we not share His concern for the vast multitudes of lost people around us?

Our Turn

Does lostness mean to us what it does to God? Does the average Christian sitting in a Sunday morning service feel God's emotions as He contemplates the eternal fate of hundreds of millions of His created ones? It is unlikely that any of us has actively tried to persuade God not to save people, "but if we do not make it possible for them to hear of His grace and power to save to the uttermost, the result is the same, as far as they are concerned."[53]

If your honest attitude toward the lost resembles Jonah's, here's a comforting thought: *There's still time.* God gave Jonah a second, third, and fourth chance to repent and adopt His heart of compassion. He doesn't just pursue us for our initial salvation. He also continues to purify and sanctify us for the rest of our lives. He wants us to understand, more and more, the true depths of the gospel we've received. And His goal isn't only to use us to minister to others, important as that is. He is also transforming us into the image of Jesus, the Son He loves (Romans 8:29, 2 Corinthians 3:18). God has His fingerprints on everything that happens in our lives. He provides us with nudges, resources, lessons, and corrections.

This is good news for negligent, self-centered Christians. While it's unlikely we have rebelled as dramatically as Jonah did or will undergo a similar mode of discipline, that doesn't mean God is not watching us. Through the highs and lows of our journey with Him, God is lovingly leading us into a deeper relationship. I like to share that thought with new outgoing missionaries. While we trust that God will use us to impact the world, another great work (and sometimes a painful one) will be going on at that same time—the sanctifying hand of God doing surgery on our own hearts.

If you want to get serious with God, there's no better way than to set out on a journey of obedience to reach those who haven't heard of the salvation and mercy He offers freely to everyone. That includes distant nations and peoples, but it also means people at work or those living next door. It's not going to be easy. God will expose our selfishness, personal agendas, values, timelines, hopes, and dreams again and again so that His loving fire can transform them. I find it's a much less painful process when I cooperate rather than resist as Jonah did.

The need for continuing learning and sanctification might be more obvious for Christians saved from more dramatic spiritual bankruptcy, like Mary Magdalene or Zacchaeus. But it's just as real for those of us raised in Christian environments or even serving in vocational ministry. We are all broken vessels in need of transformation. Some of us aren't quite as aware of how much mercy and grace we've received. Maybe we have seen ourselves as more like Jonah than the Ninevites—more prophet than pagan. But if we read the story carefully, that might mean we are inoculated against the true nature of God's love.

Seemingly "good Christians" are in danger of becoming passive-aggressive saboteurs, like sons who say, "I will," but then don't (Matthew 21:28-32), or like the older brother in Jesus' parable of the loving father, often called the story of the prodigal son (Luke 15:11-32). We have done things "right." We've played by the rules. We are resentful of God's inordinate compassion and generosity toward wayward sinners. We are like the priest and the Levite who keep our distance and pass by when we see a man lying "half dead" on the side of the road (Luke 10:25-37). And, as Jesus illustrated in another parable, it doesn't make sense to us when those who started work in the afternoon get paid just as much as those of us who've been working all day under the hot sun (Matthew 20:1-16). God's grace seems to violate justice. We are indignant and angry until we see ourselves as the recipients of His unreasonable grace.

Some people need God's grace because they are prodigals,

and others because they are self-righteous Pharisees. Both are forms of idolatry. All of us, ultimately, need the same grace. Surface-level conformity to God's instructions isn't enough. He wants heart-level transformation. Are we satisfied with following rules and going through the motions, or are we moved by His Spirit and compassion?

One of my favorite verses is 2 Chronicles 16:9, "For the eyes of the LORD range throughout the earth to strengthen those whose hearts are fully committed to him." Let's be people whose hearts are blameless and who find strong support in the God who loved the sailors and the Ninevites and the unloving prophet. Join me in praying yet another powerful prayer: "Lord, fill my heart with Your compassion."

Discussion Questions

1. Imagine for a moment that Jonah shared God's compassion for the Ninevites and celebrated their repentance. What would the next few weeks and years of his ministry have been like? What did Nineveh need, and what influence might Jonah have had?
2. Have you ever had a silent-retreat-like experience that reset your priorities? How long did the effect last?
3. Think about a time you were angry with God. Was His response anything like how He addressed Jonah?
4. Do you think the average Christian sitting in a Sunday morning service feels God's emotions as He contemplates the eternal fate of hundreds of millions of His created ones?
5. Why do you think the Holy Spirit and human writer ended the Book of Jonah the way they did?

A Continuing Story

Like a piece of delicious baklava, Jonah's story has many layers of significance and application. That's part of its genius. It stands out in the Bible because it is the only book with a persistently rebellious prophet, the only large-scale repentance of a pagan society, and the only time God gave one of His messengers an attention-grabbing voyage inside a fish. However, there is a New Testament episode that echoes some key elements of Jonah's story, minus the fish.

Echoes of Joppa

About 800 years after Jonah's adventures, we find another of God's envoys, Peter, in the port city of Joppa (Acts 10). Like Jonah, Peter is sometimes known for his "independent spirit." He ran from God and even denied his Lord three times. Mercifully recommissioned in John 21 at the Sea of Galilee, Peter is now headed in the right direction as a leader of the nascent Church.

One day, Peter is on the roof of a house in Joppa, over-looking where Jonah embarked for Tarshish centuries earlier. Suddenly, he receives instructions from God to do something he finds unthinkable. In a vision, a sheet descends from heaven filled with unclean, forbidden creatures. A voice tells him to eat them. When Peter objects that he would never eat unclean food, the voice instructs him, "Do not call anything impure that God has made clean" (Acts 10:15). The process repeats twice more, and then the vision ends. The number three, in the Hebrew mind, signifies importance and completeness. Whatever it means, this vision is a message from God.

Peter is confused, so the Holy Spirit clarifies. Messengers are coming to invite Peter to the home of Cornelius, a Roman centurion who follows God and is seeking the truth. The Spirit tells Peter to go with them without hesitation. Accepting an invitation to visit someone hardly seems extreme to us today, but it was shocking to Peter. As shocking as eating forbidden food. For centuries, Jews had considered Gentiles to be unclean. Jews didn't eat with Gentiles or enter their homes. God is asking Peter to do something he considers off-limits. How could this be what God wants?

In some important ways, Peter's experience echoes Jonah's story. Two men in different centuries receive a similar call to take a message of salvation to an unlikely and "undeserving" audience. Both have strong objections to God's plan. Jonah responds by catching a ship headed as far away as possible. Although bewildered by the vision and its implications, Peter packs his mule and obediently heads up the coast to Caesarea. Cornelius is waiting there with his entire family and circle of friends. Peter has a much more pleasant experience than Jonah since he goes voluntarily.

In both stories, the recipients of God's message have been prepared by God and are incredibly responsive. Cornelius has already shown his submission to God by sending for Peter. Before the apostle finishes his sermon, God interrupts him with another huge surprise: "While Peter was still speaking these words, the Holy Spirit came on all who heard the message. The circumcised believers who had come with Peter were astonished that the gift of the Holy Spirit had been poured out even on Gentiles. For they heard them speaking in tongues and praising God" (Acts 10:44-46).

It's as if the Spirit of God has been eagerly awaiting the arrival of a human messenger of the gospel so that He can save the extended family. Peter and his Jewish companions are amazed, but they recognize the hand of God and baptize the new believers. The events in Caesarea are so unexpected that Peter has some serious explaining to do when he returns to Jerusalem (as Jonah likely did when he reported back to Gath Hepher). But once the Apostles heard the whole story, the Jewish church "had no further objections and praised God, saying, 'So then, even to Gentiles God has granted repentance that leads to life'" (Acts 11:18). It was the beginning of a massive paradigm shift.

The bursting of the gospel reservoir out of an exclusively Jewish framework into the Gentile world was indescribably history-altering. Peter had a front-row seat to witness God do something new and wonderful, showing His love for unlikely people in an unexpected way. However reluctant he may have felt at first, Peter got to be the conduit of Abrahamic blessing, not only to Cornelius but to the entire Gentile world. When he looked back on his experience later, I'm sure he was as amazed and surprised as anyone by what God did. Following in Peter's footsteps, the Apostle Paul and many others would later flood the Roman world and beyond with the life-saving message of the gospel. Every believer today owes their salvation to Peter's door-opening obedience and the events that followed.

A Better Jonah

While God was working on Jonah, He was also using him as a mirror to illustrate the self-centeredness and obstinacy of His people, Israel. Jonah didn't just tell his story. He *was* the story. Israel had abandoned its covenantal purpose. As God's worshippers with special knowledge of Him, Abraham's heirs had been commissioned to be a blessing, not just to be blessed. By Jonah's time, Israel had been adrift for many generations. God had been patient, but time was running out. Just as Nineveh was under impending judgment, so was Israel. In fact, Nineveh's repentance showed unrepentant Israel in an even worse light.

The message of Jonah applied equally to the people of Jesus' day. In Matthew 12:38, the Pharisees and teachers of the law press Jesus for a miraculous sign to prove His credentials. They have already seen many miracles, but somehow, they aren't satisfied. Just a short time earlier, when Jesus healed a man who was both blind and mute, they blasphemously attributed it to Beelzebul, the prince of demons (Matthew 12:24). Hard-heartedly refusing to believe, they now demand another, bigger miracle. They want *irrefutable proof* that He is the promised Messiah. Jesus replies, "A wicked and adulterous generation asks for a miraculous sign! But none will be given it except the sign of the prophet Jonah" (Matthew 12:39).

What is Jesus saying here? First, Jonah's experience is a miraculous sign tailored for the hardest of hearts. Being eaten by a fish and spending three days in the ocean's depths, only to be spit out onto the beach and walk away is one of the greatest and most dramatic miracles of all time.

Secondly, Jesus is expressing in "code" that He will answer their request for a greater sign, but not in the way they expect. Jesus the Surpriser will Himself rise from the dead after three days. It will be the greatest miracle of all—far greater than Jonah's. Jonah's three days and three nights in the belly of a huge fish, it turns out, were a prophetic and symbolic foreshadowing of Jesus' death and resurrection (Matthew 12:39-40). As Jonah was "banished from [God's] sight" (Jonah 2:4) in the depths of the sea (for his rebellion), so the Messiah will soon offer to be "thrown overboard" to bear the penalty, not for His sins, but the sins of the world—"My God, my God, why have you forsaken me?" (Psalm 22:1).

The Prophet from Nazareth, just three miles from Gath Hepher, would go to a great city (Jerusalem) and weep over it. Rather than waiting outside the gates for the city's destruction, Jesus would carry His cross outside the city to save it from eternal destruction. It is the greatest real-life drama with the highest stakes and the ultimate climax. Jesus is the perfect embodiment of all Israel was intended to be and do. He embraced the Father's heart full of "amazing grace" and willingly yielded His rights for the sake of a wretched, undeserving world. Jesus is the perfect Jonah.

Jesus goes on to warn the Jewish leaders that the notorious Ninevites will one day rise at the judgment and condemn them. The wicked Assyrians repented at the preaching of

Jonah, while these arrogant leaders encountered one "greater than Jonah" and failed to repent (Matthew 12:41). Jesus declares in no uncertain terms that they are inviting an even greater punishment.

We see a clear link here between the level of light people have received and their responsibility to respond. It is intriguing that different societies and generations will testify for or against one another relative to their response and responsibility to the gospel. Jesus has already condemned Chorazin and Bethsaida, declaring that the Gentile cities of Tyre and Sidon would have repented in sackcloth and ashes if they had seen the same miracles (Matthew 11:21). The teachers of the law have encountered in Jesus a greater founder of the faith than Abraham, a truer fulfiller of the law than Moses, a supreme prophet above Elijah, and the ultimate sign beyond the testimony of Jonah, yet they have not believed. Their guilt is overflowing. The men of Nineveh will testify against them on Judgment Day.

A Message for Today

What is the core message of the book? Simply this: *Our sovereign, saving God expects us to share His heart for a lost world.*

And what are the realities and assumptions undergirding this fundamental truth? What does God teach us in the context of Jonah and his generation? Here are seven key propositions to ponder:

1. The world is in rebellion against God and, therefore, hurtling toward judgment. Most people do not realize this, but the situation is urgent.
2. God has a plan, summarized in a promise He made

to Abraham. He will bless all peoples through Jesus, Abraham's "seed." This plan involves the entire world, and nothing can stop God from accomplishing it. He is the God who saves.

3. God has a special role for His people in the plan, including you. He loves the world, but He also loves you individually. His plan for your life is superior to your own. He works patiently with you in this life-long process.

4. No one can escape God's sovereign power. The more we try, the more difficult things will get. Storms are intended to prune and prepare us. The deepest lessons are learned in the darkest places.

5. Jesus is the hero of the Great Story. He is the perfect Jonah who reflects the Father's heart and gives His life for the "great city." Everything is from, through, and for Him. God's justice and mercy have been reconciled in His finished work on the Cross.

6. God prepares people for the message He gives us. The gospel must go everywhere. Our job is to communicate it faithfully. No one is ever the same after understanding the message. It is wonderful news for those who accept it and dangerous news for those who refuse.

7. The global Church, God's people, must embrace His heart and lift our eyes to the harvest. We must stay true to our mission.

As the Book of Jonah spoke to people in generations past, it still speaks today. In many quarters of the Church, we've lost our way. We're more preoccupied with our own comfort than with the needs of a lost world. We view ourselves as spiritually erudite when, in fact, we have much to learn. We know little of true repentance or living sacrificially for the sake of the gospel. While generalizations can be dangerous, and there are many shining examples of God's faithful ones in our ranks to inspire us, we need to take stock from time to time, both personally and corporately. Pride and complacency lull us into a deep and deceptive sleep. And yet, Jesus challenges us still, "Come, follow me … and I will send you out to fish for people" (Matthew 4:19).

Today, we are experiencing the greatest spiritual harvest the world has ever known. That's exciting but also creates a massive need for harvest workers. It is time for all hands to be "on deck." There are many roles to play. It's time for the whole body of Christ to be mobilized. Do we leave room for God's surprises in our prayers and plans? Maybe He is calling us out of Gath Hepher, our comfort zones, to a Nineveh that needs to know things we have known for a long time. Will we respond like Peter or like Jonah? Let's live sacrificially for the one thing that matters in eternity: the glory of God through the advancement of Christ's kingdom.

When God gave Abraham the "original" Great Commission 4,000 years ago, He revealed His game plan for the present age. What are we doing as stewards of that tremendous treasure? I believe God is setting aside some of us for very direct, front-line roles, including reaching the 7,000 unreached people groups in the world today. Most of us will play essential support roles, giving, praying, and encouraging our brothers and sisters who obediently leave Joppa for the regions beyond while we carry out the same mission in our own circles of influence. All of us should pray with a posture of openness and expectation. We might not get instructions as clear as Jonah's or Peter's, but we can all take steps of obedience as God gives us faith and opportunity.

I hope you will join me in worshiping God as the Great Surpriser. Be on the lookout for unanticipated things He may do in your life. I often voice the prayer of Psalm 67: "Lord, bless the nations through me." That's a prayer God loves to answer.

Discussion Questions

1. What parallels do you see between Jonah's and Peter's experiences in Joppa? What was different about their circumstances and responses?
2. How well does the summary statement, *Our sovereign, saving God expects us to share His heart for a lost world,* capture the message of the Book of Jonah? Which of the seven propositions under "A Message for Today" resonate the most? Which do you find challenging?
3. How are you already participating in God's mission of mercy to the world? Are you fully "on board?" If not, what's holding you back?
4. What steps of obedience can you take this week to deepen or expand your involvement in God's global mission? What questions do you have? Who can you talk to about your concerns and ideas?
5. In your prayers and plans, how can you leave room for God's surprises?

Acknowledgments

I'm forever grateful to Maxine McDonald for helping me tirelessly with this project and to Shelly Kearns, Carol Richardson, Marti Wade, and Matt Green for their refining textual touches.

Notes

Introduction

1. "Gettysburg Address," *Britannica,* https://www.britannica.com/event/Gettysburg-Address, April 17, 2024.
2. JoAnna M. Hoyt, *Amos, Jonah, and Micah, Evangelical Exegetical Commentary* (Bellingham, Wash.: Lexham Press, 2018), 406-408, Logos.

Chapter 1: A Surprising God

3. The story is told in Chapter 19 of *Peace Child,* by Don Richardson (Minneapolis, Minn.: Bethany House, 2005).
4. Judson Mather, "The Comic Act of the Book of Jonah," *Soundings* 65, Fall 1982, 283. Quoted in John D. Hannah, "Jonah," in *The Bible Knowledge Commentary: An Exposition of the Scriptures by Dallas Seminary Faculty, Old Testament,* ed. by John F. Walvoord and Roy B. Zuck (Wheaton, Ill.: Victor Books, 1985), 1472.
5. Hoyt, *Amos, Jonah, and Micah,* 339, Logos.
6. Hobart E. Freeman, *An Introduction to the Old Testament Prophets* (Chicago: Moody, 1968), 1980 printing, 165-166.
7. Phil Johnson, "Jonah Overview—Phil Johnson," Exposit the Word, YouTube video, 50:05,

September 13, 2019, https://www.youtube.com/
watch?v=SoVgjl0BEv4&t=1877s.

8. Ibid.

9. Charles L. Feinberg, *The Minor Prophets* (Chicago, Ill.:
Moody Press, 2013), 134. Formerly published in the
series Major Messages of the Minor Prophets, Jonah,
Micah, and Nahum in 1951, fifth printing in 1980.

10. John D. Hannah, "Jonah," in *The Bible Knowledge Commentary: An Exposition of the Scriptures
by Dallas Seminary Faculty, Old Testament,* ed. by
John F. Walvoord and Roy B. Zuck (Wheaton, Ill.:
Victor Books, 1985), 1462.

11. 42.5 percent of the world's population is considered
unreached according to "Global Dashboard," Joshua
Project, https://joshuaproject.net, accessed June 6, 2024.

Chapter 2: An Unthinkable Mission

12. Johnson, "Jonah Overview—Phil Johnson."

13. Hannah, "Jonah," 1464.

14. Johnson, "Jonah Overview—Phil Johnson."

15. "City and Town Population Totals: 2020-2022," US
Census Bureau, June 3, 2023, https://www.census.
gov/data/tables/time-series/demo/popest/2020s-total-
cities-and-towns.html.

16. W. Graham Scroggie, *The Unfolding Drama of Redemp-
tion, vol 1: The Prologue and Act I of the Drama
Embracing the Old Testament* (Grand Rapids, Mich.:
Kregel Publications, 1994), 383.

17. "Wall Panel; Relief," The British Museum, https://www.

britishmuseum.org/collection/object/W_1851-0902-7-a, accessed April 12, 2024.

18. C. F. Keil and F. Delitzsch, *Commentary on the Old Testament, vol 10: Minor Prophets,* trans. by James Martin (Peabody, Mass.: Hendrickson, 1996), 264, Logos.

19. Hoyt, *Amos, Jonah, and Micah,* 415, Logos.

20. Phil Johnson, "Jonah—Love Poured Out Like Water—Phil Johnson," Exposit the Word, YouTube video, 47:30, September 13, 2019, https://www.youtube.com/watch?v=FKVF03Fd-5c&t=3s.

21. Keil and Delitzsch, *Commentary on the Old Testament,* 264, Logos.

22. Don Richardson, *Peace Child* (Minneapolis, Minn.: Bethany House, 2005).

23. "Share of the population living in urbanized areas," Our World in Data, January 2, 2024, https://ourworldindata.org/grapher/urbanization-last-500-years.

24. Einar H. Dyvik, "Degree of urbanization 2023, by continent," Statista, January 9, 2024, https://www.statista.com/statistics/270860/urbanization-by-continent.

Chapter 3: An Unlikely Conscript

25. Brian Stanley, "Winning the world: Carey and the modern missionary movement," Christian History Institute, originally published in *Christian History* Issue #9 in 1984, https://christianhistoryinstitute.org/magazine/article/winning-the-world-carey-and-modern-missions, accessed June 7, 2024.

26. "William Carey: Father of modern Protestant missions,"

Christianity Today, https://www.christianitytoday.com/history/people/missionaries/william-carey.html, accessed June 7, 2024.

27. Hoyt, *Amos, Jonah, and Micah,* 404, Logos.
28. Feinberg, *The Minor Prophets,* 135.
29. Hoyt, *Amos, Jonah, and Micah,* 417, Logos.
30. Ibid., 443, Logos.
31. Ibid.
32. Elinor Young, *Running on Broken Legs: My Journey to Joy* (Enumclaw, Wash.: Redemption Press, 2022), 51.
33. United Bible Societies, "Indonesia's Kimyal people welcome the New Testament," YouTube video, 6:05, June 28, 2012, https://www.youtube.com/watch?v=BmbTFo1cR6I.
34. Dianne Becker, "'Bad Legs' – Elinor, a Missionary Story," YouTube video, 22:46, June 15, 2015, https://www.youtube.com/watch?v=PuRvXePv_wA.
35. About two-thirds of the people in the world are not Christians. Eighty percent of them do not know a Christian according to "Status of Global Christianity, 2023, in the Context of 1900–2050," Center for the Study of World Christianity at Gordon-Conwell Theological Seminary, https://www.gordonconwell.edu/wp-content/uploads/sites/13/2023/01/Status-of-Global-Christianity-2023.pdf, accessed June 6, 2024. Based on Todd M. Johnson and Gina A. Zurlo, eds. World Christian Database (Leiden/Boston: Brill), www.worldchristiandatabase.org, accessed January 2023.
36. "Global Dashboard," Joshua Project, https://joshuaproject.net, accessed June 6, 2024.

37. "Frontier Unreached People Groups," Joshua Project, https://joshuaproject.net/frontier, accessed April 12, 2024.

Chapter 4: An Extraordinary Response

38. Feinberg, *The Minor Prophets*, 136.
39. Hoyt, *Amos, Jonah, and Micah*, 444, Logos.
40. Ibid., 443-444, Logos.
41. Hannah, "Jonah," 1462.
42. Feinberg, *The Minor Prophets*, 144.
43. Ibid., 144-145.
44. Ibid., 146.
45. Hannah, "Jonah," 1470.
46. Don Richardson, *Eternity in Their Hearts* (Minneapolis, Minn.: Bethany House, 1981).
47. "Time Traveling Plants," Arizona State University Ask a Biologist, https://askabiologist.asu.edu/content/how-long-can-seeds-live-underground, accessed April 12, 2024.
48. Jae Kyeong Lee, "South Korea's Great Missionary Movement—God's Sovereignty, Our Obedience," International Mission Board, February 9, 2018, https://www.imb.org/2018/02/09/south-korea-mission-movement/.

Chapter 5: A Merciless Missionary

49. Lucy Kafanov, "NFL star Aaron Rodgers went to a darkness retreat to contemplate his future. What is that and how does it work?" CNN, https://www.cnn.com/2023/02/26/us/aaron-rodgers-darkness-retreat-wellness-ctpr/index.html, February 27, 2023.

50. Executive Committee of the Editorial Board and
    J. Frederic McCurdy, "Nineveh," Jewish Ency-
    clopedia, https://www.jewishencyclopedia.com/
    articles/11549-nineveh, accessed June 13, 2024.
51. Feinberg, *The Minor Prophets,* 148.
52. Hannah, "Jonah," 1473.
53. Feinberg, *The Minor Prophets,* 152.

If you enjoyed *Not on Board*, please consider leaving a review on Amazon. This helps more people discover the book.

Looking for more missions content like this?

Check out Steve's book *Is the Commission Still Great? Eight Myths About Missions and What They Mean for the Church.*

Printed in the USA
CPSIA information can be obtained
at www.ICGtesting.com
LVHW041459141024
793784LV00032B/385

9 781735 234564